Dear k

Welcome to the
WBJ team! We
are thrilled to
have you. Enjoy
these stories :)

Cheers,

Jennifer

Also by Jennifer Stanton

5 Steps to Expert Wine Tasting

A Sommelier's Quick Reference Guide to Wine Regions and Styles

#PinotKitty: A Cat's Life

A Sommelier's Quick Reference Guide to Wine Grape Varietals from around the World

Wines by Jennifer® Cookbook, First Edition

Wines by Jennifer® Cookbook, Second Edition

Top 10 Mistakes Wine Country Travelers Make and How to Avoid Them

The Wines by Jennifer® Story

How I Created a Dream Lifestyle Business That Helps People <u>Just Like You</u> Enjoy an Authentic Global Wine Country Experience!

Jennifer Stanton

Lopez Publishing, LLC

First paperback edition 2018
First eBook edition 2018

Second paperback edition 2020
Second eBook edition 2020

Cover photo credit: Dr. Greg Rose
Cover design by WordPictures KC

ISBN 978-1-7328501-2-5 (paperback)
ISBN 978-1-7328501-3-2 (eBook)

Published by Lopez Publishing, LLC 2020

www.WinesByJennifer.com

Dedication

This book is dedicated to our beloved Wines by Jennifer® mascot, #PinotKitty.

Feline *bon vivant*, author, official customer welcoming committee, social media darling, WBJ® Wine Garden security detail, and captor of our hearts since 2004, the shoppe just wouldn't be the same without him.

Table of Contents

Introduction.. i

Acknowledgments.................................... ii

Part One: In the Beginning

    1. The Catalyst................................. 3

    2. Not Our First Rodeo......................... 6

    3. The Birth of a Brand........................ 12

Part Two: Success Leaves Clues

    4. The Turning Point........................... 27

    5. The Secret Sauce........................... 35

    6. Innovators................................. 45

    7. We're Working!............................. 62

Part Three: Here to Stay

    8. We've Arrived.............................. 71

9. Ichiro & Emiko............................ 84

10. Doing Well by Doing Good................ 92

Part Four: The Travel

11. Global Vagabonds........................... 97

12. Fifty before 50™............................... 103

13. Playing "The Game"........................ 132

Part Five: The Future

14. When Everyone's Zigging,
    It's Time to Zag............................ 151

Additional Resources............................... 155

Index.. 156

Introduction

Wines by Jennifer® is a unique luxury entertainment destination that has been helping people enjoy an authentic global wine country experience in historic downtown Parkville, Missouri since 2003.

Following are stories, experiences, anecdotes, and memories collected over the last 18 years spent living the dream.

Acknowledgments

Just as no man is an island, neither is any successful business.

Many have selflessly contributed to our success all these years, but I would like to give special recognition to our Wines by Jennifer® team members, both past and present, to whom we owe a great deal of our success.

The stories you are about to read would not have been possible were it not for their commitment and dedication to us, the shoppe, and our customers, especially during our frequent and extended absences.

For that, they all have our enduring gratitude.

Part One

IN THE BEGINNING

1 The Catalyst

Any American of a certain age can easily remember exactly where they were and what they were doing on that fateful day of Tuesday, September 11th, 2001. I am no exception.

As it was in New York City, Washington, D.C., and over a field in western Pennsylvania, the day dawned with gorgeous, crystal-clear skies and comfortable late-summer temperatures in Kansas City. It was the kind of day we pilots refer to as "CAVU," meaning "ceiling and visibility unlimited." In other words, an absolutely perfect day to fly, which is exactly what both I and my significant other (later husband) Don intended to do.

I was scheduled for an instrument proficiency check flight with my dear friend, flight instructor, and veteran B-24 captain, Perry Perez, in the new (to us) Mooney M20J Don and I had just purchased. Meanwhile, Don was busy making plans to deliver an airplane from Portland, Maine to Greenville, South Carolina for Bill

Perry of Maine Beechcraft, a regular customer of our aircraft ferry business, Select Air Group, Inc.

Perry and I met that morning as scheduled at the downtown Kansas City airport where we hangared our new bird, and I quickly got to work with my usual pre-flight checklist activities.

After launching the flight, Perry and I headed west toward Topeka, Kansas, where he began putting me through my instrument paces with help from our friends at air traffic control (ATC).

But what had been a routine day of air work up to that point suddenly began to change.

It all started when Perry and I both noticed the controllers taking on a heightened sense of urgency. They were giving very unconventional instructions to the aircraft they were controlling, and we saw aircraft out our cockpit window entering random holding patterns and conducting other odd flight maneuvers.

What we later learned was happening was a feverish attempt by ATC to comply with an unprecedented emergency order issued by FAA Command Center in Herndon, Virginia to ground all 4,000+ commercial airline flights following the attacks on the World Trade Center and the Pentagon, effective immediately.

The Catalyst

Countless general aviation flights such as ours were being grounded on the spot as well, but thanks to Perry's foresight, he immediately had me point the Mooney back to Kansas City. This was a move that, along with our very cooperative controller, saved us from a similar fate.

I was busy trying to process all this activity in my head but still keeping foremost in my mind the "golden rule" of flying in stressful situations that Perry had drilled into me so many times before: "Aviate, navigate, communicate." In other words, I had to focus first and foremost on maintaining positive control of my aircraft to keep us safe.

But from his 60+ years of instructor experience, much of it spent in the military, Perry had already figured it out...

"Jennifer, America is under attack."

2 Not Our First Rodeo

Actually, Wines by Jennifer® was not the first business Don and I created together. Before that, there was our aircraft ferry business, Select Air Group, Inc., which we literally created on a napkin while sitting poolside over a bottle of wine one summer Sunday in 2000.

You see, Don and I are both commercial pilots, which is an advanced certification that permits you to fly "for hire."

I like to describe the basic private pilot certificate as a bachelor's degree, while the commercial certificate would be the equivalent of a master's degree. The very top of the pilot food chain is the Airline Transport Pilot (ATP) certificate, which would be the PhD level. We haven't achieved that (yet).

We had long wanted to take advantage of that status and actually get paid to fly. Don in particular was excited at the prospect, as he comes from a long line of professional aviators and was eager to keep the family tradition alive.

So while his bachelor's degree in Aviation Technology from the University of Central Missouri may have provided the inspiration, it was his avid study of direct response marketing that provided the perspiration, and led to the creation of our company.

Claude Hopkins, John Caples, Eugene Schwartz, Victor Schwab, David Ogilvie, Robert Collier, and Richard Benson were just names on Don's bookshelf back then, but I now know those direct response titans provided the foundation for his self-directed marketing education that has served us and our businesses so well both then and now.

Dan Kennedy, Ken McCarthy, and Brian Kurtz were among the contemporary names I also became familiar with through his studies. Now it's like we're all old friends.

But, back to airplanes.

Just like in real estate, the airplane business has brokers that buy and sell assets. In this case, the assets are mobile, and they need to be transported from one location to another.

That's where ferry pilots come in.

Utilizing some of the direct response techniques he had learned from his studies, Don thought it would be a good approach to run what he called "space ads" in industry publications with our offer and see what happened.

So that's what we did.

We had several benefits we could provide over other aircraft ferry businesses around at the time, namely:

- We had our own aircraft, which provided us much more utility.

- As entrepreneurs, we had flexible schedules that allowed us to respond "on demand."

- Don had "buddy passes" from his days in the airline industry, allowing him to travel to and from the aircraft locations at little cost.

There's an axiom in business that you can't have good, fast, and cheap, but in this case, we had all three.

The response from the space ads was exciting to see!

In short order, we had three brokers across the country sign on as customers sending us a steady stream of business: one in California, one in Ohio, and one in Maine.

This geographic distribution proved to be quite convenient. Like putting together pieces of a puzzle, with a little creativity we were able to coordinate multiple aircraft movements in a single trip. Furthermore, I was able to work in visits to my clients in the energy trading business along the way for maximum efficiency.

For example, on one occasion Don and I were able to move five aircraft for two different customers while I called on three separate clients in a single 7-day stretch.

How's that for efficiency?

Word travels fast in the aircraft broker world, so it wasn't long before we started getting other requests for more sophisticated missions. From tailwheels to turbines, we were getting orders faster than we could fulfill them.

Not being in the business of turning away customers, we went to work figuring out how to satisfy all the requests we were getting.

Turns out it wasn't that difficult, because who do pilots hang out with? That's right, other pilots.

And what do all pilots want to do? They want to fly!

So we started tapping into our network, and began to distribute missions selectively to other pilots who were qualified and available to fly the missions we couldn't.

It was easy. Sign some paperwork, keep a small cut for ourselves, and make both our pilots and customers happy.

Win, win, win.

Our little hobby business that started on a napkin was suddenly growing leaps and bounds in customers, missions, and pilots.

We were flying more than ever, and even making a little money while we were at it.

Life was good, right?

It was, indeed, right up until 9/11.

As unnerving and emotional as September 11th was for all Americans, it was a double whammy for Don and me. That's because it also delivered a significant gut-punch to our thriving aircraft ferry business.

Commercial aviation was obviously one of the most adversely affected sectors of American industry following those devastating events. Aircraft were grounded, pilots were stranded, the skies were eerily silent, security was Code Red, and public confidence was significantly shaken.

Yet as challenging as the situation was for the airlines, general aviation (GA) was hit even harder. The doubt and uncertainty surrounding the future of GA in this country meant buyers stopped buying and brokers stopped selling.

And airplanes stopped moving.

It was, in other words, the "perfect storm" of adversity for our fledgling business.

3 The Birth of a Brand

In all honesty, I had been considering a change in my life even before 9/11.

My whole career had been spent in the corporate world, and I had seen the worst of it from all sides.

Growing up professionally in that environment, there were many things I either barely tolerated, or didn't tolerate at all:

- the corporate backstabbing and political maneuvering

- the endless meetings seemingly held only for the purpose of scheduling another meeting

- the dysfunction and inefficiency

- the cubicles and empty suits

- the mismanagement that bordered on executive malpractice

And it wasn't any prettier when I graduated to the other side of the table.

When I was chosen as VP/GM for a subsidiary of a Fortune 150 company (their very first female ever in that role), I became accountable for all sales and operations across 22 Midwestern states.

So now I was the one running the show. But with that authority came the responsibility for making the tough decisions:

- managing instability and uncertainty during mergers and acquisitions

- gutting business units to rid them of incompetence

- reporting to boards of directors I had no hand in selecting

At the end of the day, it was still just as unsatisfying, unfulfilling, stressful, and frustrating.

I knew things were bad when even the travel was getting me down! While Don was thankfully always there to pick up the slack, I felt guilty and upset to be missing out on all our son Daniel's activities.

His athletic career was just starting to get into full swing, and Don was busy coaching both him and his teams. But all I could do was listen to second-hand reports over the phone while spending another night alone in another sterile hotel room in another boring town.

My son was basically growing up without me. Even our dogs barely recognized me when I got home.

And for what? Although I was being handsomely compensated, I still felt like I was working only to further someone else's agenda and pad someone else's bank account.

I was so sick of it all, and I knew something had to change. Besides, I thought to myself, if all else fails, I can always go get another job.

I had already had a taste of successful private enterprise with Select Air Group, and I wanted more of that. I wanted to create something where I would be in total and complete control of my own destiny.

Success would be my success, or failure would be my failure.

So, in my mind, the question of "why" had been emphatically answered.

"Where" and "when" were also easy: "here" and "now."

The only questions remaining were the more challenging ones of "what" and "how."

It's a rare day that goes by that I don't hear some variation on the following:

- *"How did Wines by Jennifer get started?"*
- *"Where did you come up with this idea?"*
- *"We've never seen anything like this anywhere!"*

The irony is that Wines by Jennifer® was actually supposed to be a bed-and-breakfast.

The story began in the early 1990s during my corporate days. I was spending considerable time on a project in Hutchinson, Kansas, where I occasionally would stay at Hedrick's, an exotic animal farm that was also home to a bed-and-breakfast.

It was quite a place (and still is today): zebras playing with camels, ostriches wandering among giraffes and kangaroos, and other critters that seemed totally out of place on the Kansas prairie.

Interestingly enough, all of the rooms there are themed after these different animals, with a décor to match. I loved that idea, and made a point to stay in a different room each time so I could experience them all.

Fast forward a few years to the mid-90s, shortly after Daniel was born. It was at that time that I began to envision flying him and myself around the world after his high school graduation in our very own King Air twin turboprop aircraft. We would stop at whatever countries along the route that captured our interest.

I even went so far as to meet with my financial advisor and develop formal plans for accomplishing this goal, plans which I still have to this day.

When the trip was completed and Daniel went off to college, my next move would be to open a bed-and-breakfast with an airstrip that would be marketed and made available exclusively to pilots.

And inspired by my time at Hedrick's, all of the rooms at my b-and-b would be themed after the different countries Daniel and I had visited on our around-the-world adventure.

But Don, whom I had met in 1999, was never a fan of this plan.

Bed-and-breakfasts seemed like way too much work, he argued, with way too little reward, and virtually no time off. I had to agree that it probably would not be conducive to the extensive world traveling we had envisioned for ourselves.

So, in early 2002, I began to look for other opportunities.

I had long had a love of food and wine. I came from a long line of chefs and wine lovers, and my parents were proud owners of an extensive wine cellar. As a matter of fact, when they retired to Hot Springs, Arkansas in 1998, I was actively involved in the inventory reduction of said cellar to help make their move more manageable.

The sacrifices we make for our loved ones!

After they got settled in Hot Springs, I would visit frequently, and those visits often included trips to the local Arkansas wineries. My dad would often joke that I should buy a vineyard and make him some wine, but I always teased back that maybe *he* should buy the vineyard *for me*, then I would make him some wine.

Even back in my corporate days, anywhere I traveled I would always manage to work in a trip to the local wine country, if it existed.

But the sad reality was that I would invariably be disappointed when I returned home to Kansas City, because absolutely nothing remotely like that was available there at the time.

Then, suddenly the idea struck me like a bolt out of the blue:

Why don't I create my own business based upon the exact "wine country experience" I wished already existed that would allow me to escape Corporate America and indulge my passion at the same time?!

I could design and create this new "wine country experience" just the way I wanted, complete with my beloved "themed rooms" concept. Each room throughout this shoppe would just represent a different wine region instead.

My "eureka" moment had arrived!

Without even really realizing it at the time, I had just conceived Wines by Jennifer® in my mind by utilizing a proven technique for creating a successful business: identify a hole in the market and find a way to fill it.

As excited as I was about my new venture, I still thought some validation of the idea might be in order to help determine just how big this "hole" might be. So I called upon long-time friend, fellow aviator, and liquor industry veteran, Marshall Rimann, and invited him to lunch to run the concept by him.

His positive feedback and encouragement after hearing about my idea was just the little push I needed to dive headlong into the project.

Now I just needed a location. Fortunately, I had a secret weapon in this process.

Don had earned his broker license from the Missouri Real Estate Commission in 1994, so I was in very good hands with this piece of the puzzle. He had plenty of contacts and knowledge from nearly a decade of experience running his own successful real estate business. This gave me great confidence in our ability to get the location issue resolved to our satisfaction.

Don and I began scouting areas around our home in Parkville, figuring that if I was going to be spending significant amounts of time at this new venture, it might as well be close to home.

But more importantly, we also knew from extensive market research that the Parkville area was growing in both size and affluence, two trends that fit nicely with the "dream lifestyle business" I intended to create.

That was all well and good, but try as we might, our search results were coming up empty. Lead after lead turned into dead end after dead end, and frustration was mounting.

Then, inspiration struck again.

I had a college friend, Jay Harms, who was an entrepreneur with a successful business in downtown Parkville. On a complete whim, I gave him a call to see if he might be able to help.

As luck would have it, Jay mentioned that his business partner had a property on Main Street that he was just preparing for rent. Would I be interested to talk to him?

Yes, please!

A successful businessman in his own right, Mark Coulter owned several properties in downtown Parkville, and he proved to be just the ally I needed.

Mark loved my concept, and was very cooperative during our lease discussions. Being a wine lover himself, he really wanted to see the concept succeed, too.

One very important detail in our negotiation came as a result of Don's expertise. We requested and were granted a purchase option in the lease that gave us control of the underlying real estate, an option we ultimately exercised.

We shook hands on an agreement that was tentative in nature, because there was one obstacle remaining: convince the Parkville aldermen that my concept was appropriate for Main Street Parkville.

Not a slam dunk by any stretch.

It would be necessary for me to personally present my idea at the next Parkville alderman meeting, which was just a few days away. I contacted City Hall, got myself on the agenda, and hurriedly began my preparations.

But first, I decided to play a little trick I had up my sleeve!

I had a group of friends at the time (one of whom is actually a valuable member of our team today) that would meet periodically to enjoy food and wine together. Secretly, I organized our next get-together for the very night I was to present to the aldermen.

At first, it was business as usual as the group gathered at our home. But shortly after everyone had arrived, I excused myself to take care of a pressing "issue" that had arisen.

Back in those days, the Parkville alderman meetings were televised on the local public access station. Don was in on the ruse, so he stayed home to turn on the TV (back when we had one) at the appointed time when I was to appear on the agenda to surprise my friends.

Surprise was an understatement.

Although I didn't see it personally, Don said the girls' reactions were priceless:

"Look, there's Jennifer on TV!"

"What in the world is she doing?!"

"Oh my gosh, she's gonna open a wine boutique!"

"Go, Jennifer, go!!"

Well, that indeed was my plan, but first there was still that little detail about convincing the aldermen.

Although I didn't realize it at the time, I was fortunate that there were a few wine lovers in the group. They championed my cause, and used all their powers of persuasion in attempting to convert the skeptics.

Finally, after a vote that was closer than I care to recall, I was granted conditional approval to pursue my dream of creating what is now known as Wines by Jennifer®!

Many of those aldermen that originally endorsed my concept became WBJ® club members when I opened, and most have remained staunch supporters ever since. I am extremely grateful to them all for helping me make my dream come true.

So having successfully crossed the final hurdle, I hustled back home to celebrate over some bubbly with Don and my friends.

And the rest, as they say, is history.

Part Two

SUCCESS LEAVES CLUES

4 The Turning Point

There was actually a point in time when Wines by Jennifer® as we know it today almost ceased to exist, but not for the reasons you might think.

Only two people ever knew how close that came to actually happening: Don and me.

Until now.

In fact, if it weren't for Don talking me down "off the ledge" one day in his office, well, it is quite likely you would not be reading this book right now.

Rewind, if you will, all the way back to 2005, the third year of operation for Wines by Jennifer®.

Business was great and the shoppe was prospering, but I was struggling under the weight of its success.

Like a lot of start-up businesses, most of my team members at the time consisted of friends and family. They were instrumental in helping me get Wines by Jennifer® up and running, particularly my sister

Gretchen and her husband Darrell, but now they all were understandably ready to move on with their lives.

I had been fortunate to find two very valuable assets, the husband-wife team of Al and Teri Szalay. Or more accurately, they found me. They visited as customers on Day One, transitioned to team members shortly thereafter, and believe it or not, they never left — thank goodness!

But it wasn't enough.

I was looking for ways to relieve the pressure. I had thought about closing the shoppe entirely to the public and turning it into a pure event space. No retail, no tasting room, no nothing, just private events.

But my conscience wouldn't allow it. I couldn't turn my back on the loyal following I had built to that point.

So I continued to look for alternatives.

Although Don had been involved with the shoppe from the beginning, it was much more of a supporting role in those days. After helping during the facility build-out and the preparation leading to our grand opening, his involvement was limited to website maintenance, periodic marketing initiatives, wine deliveries to our legacy club members, and the occasional cameo appearance working shifts "on the floor."

It wasn't his fault – after all, he had his own "dream lifestyle business" to run.

After 10 years in South Florida, Don had moved back to Kansas City in 1994 to help care for his ailing mother.

He held stock options from a start-up company he helped build back in Florida that had just gone public, so he was evaluating business opportunities. Having always been interested in real estate, he decided to start a brokerage firm specializing in helping investors.

Investment activity was strong, and his business, Freedom Properties, quickly took off. In the meantime, he was steadily building his own real estate portfolio based upon a solid strategy he had devised.

His plan was centered around accumulating both commercial and residential properties, taking advantage of the low interest rate environment by putting all his mortgages on 15-year notes.

He would focus on taking good care of his "customers," which is what he considered his tenants to be, while they would faithfully pay off his mortgages and then some with their rent checks each month.

Then, in just a few short years, he would own a large inventory of income-producing properties completely free and clear.

A great plan being well executed, but it wasn't helping me.

I was still spending long days followed by late nights pouring wine, preparing food, washing dishes, and receiving and stocking products. (At least I still had the more glamorous tasks of cleaning toilets, dusting shelves, and sweeping floors!)

And because I was not far removed from my days as a C-level executive, I still had fresh memories of wining and dining my C-level clients with a large expense account while people took care of *me.*

Plus, I was *still* missing most of Daniel's events, because I haven't even mentioned the off-hours responsibilities of accounting and marketing and payroll and government reporting and on and on and on.

Don't be fooled, small business can be messy and it can be hard.

But at that stage, I hadn't really even created a small business yet, I had created a job. The operation was a work in progress that wasn't completely dialed in yet.

The truth of the matter was, despite all its success, I was second-guessing my decision to open the shoppe.

So, back to that meeting…

I came down to Don's office where he was working, weary and frustrated after another in a long line of late nights at the shoppe. Frankly, I had had enough.

I told him that I had reached my breaking point, and unless he had any better ideas, I was ready to close down the shoppe.

It's not an overstatement to say that the fate of Wines by Jennifer® hung on his response.

"Hold on, hold on," he said. "Let's talk this through first."

Don already understood the virtues of the shoppe, and he was quick to remind me of them:

- *an exciting, fast-paced, dream lifestyle business*

- *a lively environment full of happy people having fun*

- *a profitable operation despite being open just 40 hours per week*

- *and the big one...drinking on the job*

(Just kidding—although we taste plenty of wine, beer, and spirits as part of our job, in this business, a spittoon is your friend!)

But he fully appreciated my aggravation and frustration, too, having been on the receiving end of both a time or two.

So after a brief pause that to me seemed like an eternity, Don volunteered what he thought might be a solution.

Because he had organized his business to the point where it nearly ran on autopilot, he had some spare time on his hands. What if he began to get more involved at Wines by Jennifer®, both on the scene and behind the scenes?

I thought he'd never ask!

I quickly accepted his offer, and that's when Wines by Jennifer® really began to take off.

Whereas before it was primarily a retail wine shoppe with a tasting room, it was soon to develop into the dynamic enterprise full of multiple moving parts and components that it is today.

Don and I have extremely complementary skill sets, but both are firmly grounded in the fundamentals of sales and marketing, operations, and customer service.

Don brought a strong management background from his days as the station administrator for Eastern Airlines at Ft. Lauderdale-Hollywood International Airport. In that role, he directed a staff of managers and employees who carried out airport operations at Eastern's fifth-largest station in the world.

He also had experience in the private sector from his time spent as executive director at a group medical practice of OB/GYNs in South Florida, where he had full authority and responsibility for everything non-medical. While there, he led an expansion that saw office locations double from two to four, and production capacity significantly increased by the addition of ancillary providers such as nurse-practitioners and nurse-midwives.

He had great success improving the overall efficiency and profitability of the practice, and I know he attributes much of his business acumen to working with this very savvy group of physicians.

I, on the other hand, had extensive experience in sales and marketing.

The process began with my formal education at Northwest Missouri State University, where I earned a Master in Business Administration with an emphasis in marketing, and was also a published marketing author.

The journey continued in my early professional career when I sold multi-million dollar mainframe computers for Burroughs, which later merged with Sperry and became Unisys.

Finally, the circle was completed when I began to teach what I had learned as an adjunct marketing instructor at Park University in Parkville.

So naturally, in a complete role reversal, today I handle all the administration and Don runs the marketing for Wines by Jennifer®! I think maybe we were both just looking for a new challenge, but it's comforting to know we always have each other as a resource.

Meanwhile, Daniel, having grown into the business over the years, is now fully immersed and largely running the day-to-day operation of the shoppe, a role he has assumed with aplomb.

Because Don and I were (and still are) students of Napoleon Hill's classic self-help book, Think and Grow Rich, we were both very familiar with the mastermind concept. But it wasn't until we began to personally witness the power of two (and now with Daniel, three) minds working together toward a common goal — the growth of the Wines by Jennifer® brand — that we fully appreciated this synergy.

Our whole truly *is* greater than the sum of our parts!

5 The Secret Sauce

I am often asked how we do what we do. The "secret sauce," if you will.

The secret is that there is no secret. It's hiding in plain sight.

And I am about to share it with you now.

It's about creating and fostering a *culture*:

- A culture based on serving *people*.

- And a culture based on having *fun*.

Because that's the whole point of our business: helping people have fun.

Kansas City-based wine expert Doug Frost is one of only four people on the planet with the dual credentials of Master Sommelier and Master of Wine, making him one of the foremost authorities in the world on the business of wine. He recently observed that, to have success in the wine business, you've got to have "service in your bones."

I'll take that even a step further.

To have success in *any* business, you've got to have service in your bones. Because at the end of the day, it's always about *helping* people.

And by people, I don't mean just customers.

I mean team members, vendors, and virtually anybody else we come into contact with, too.

Our goal is to have an all-inclusive "people first" mentality that permeates the entire organization. It should be both generous and transparent, but most importantly, it must start at the top.

If it does, then it has no choice but to flow first to our team, and ultimately to our customers. And if it doesn't, then we're not providing customer service, we're providing lip service.

Our service-driven culture also translates well to what is another pillar of our success, word of mouth referrals, or what one of Don's mentors, Ken McCarthy, calls "buzz" marketing.

And to ensure that the customer receives the personalized "wow" experience in a beautiful, clean environment that facilitates "buzz" referrals, our crackerjack team is empowered and given explicit instructions to make customer-driven decisions based upon our modified version of the Golden Rule, which is:

"Do unto others not as you would have done unto you. Do unto others as you determine <u>they</u> would have done unto themselves."

In other words, the first order of business is to ask:

"What does the customer want?"

The second order of business then is to ask:

"What do we have to offer that helps them get what they want?"

Quite honestly, sometimes we don't have an answer for that second question.

And that's ok, too, because it's impossible to be all things to all people.

The Wines by Jennifer® Story

I've always heeded what I consider sage advice from famous management consultant Peter Drucker, who said, "Culture eats strategy for breakfast."

But I also happen to believe that if you can own *both*, you can own your market. Because to me, culture *plus* strategy eats *competitors* for breakfast.

Or makes them largely irrelevant. Either way.

In other words, being *customer*-focused eliminates any need to be *competitor*-focused.

So many business people waste valuable time constantly looking in their rearview mirror worrying about who's chasing them. Or more likely, peering out the front windshield to see *who they're chasing*.

Not us.

Our days are too filled with studying, learning, and implementing new ways to help people to worry about what others are doing.

We keep the focus squarely where it belongs, on the customer. When that happens, everything else falls right into place.

Every. Single. Time.

Speaking of culture, what doesn't work, in my opinion, is a culture based on "no."

I need look no further for an example of this than an establishment we visited while on the West Coast writing this book.

Upon arrival, the signs were everywhere.

"No" this, "no" that, "don't" this, "don't" that.

With apologies to Five Man Electrical Band, it was nothing but *do this, don't do that, can't you read the signs?"*

We also had what we considered a reasonable special request, responded to with a resounding "no."

Alrighty then...

I ask you, is that an environment conducive to a good experience?

Finally! A question where "no" is the correct response.

Instead, we have worked very intentionally to make Wines by Jennifer® a culture of "Yes":

39

The Wines by Jennifer® Story

- *Can we do a wine tasting? Yes!*

- *Can we do a wine flight? Yes!*

- *Can we open a bottle of wine? Yes!*

- *Can we take it to go? Yes!*

- *Can I enjoy a glass of sparkling? Yes!*

- *Can we have a glass of white? Yes!*

Noticing a trend?

- *Can we do a glass of rosé? Yes!*

- *Can we do a glass of red? Yes!*

- *Can we have a glass of sweet wine? Yes!*

- *Can I have a beer? Yes!*

- *Do you have spirits? Yes!*

- *Can we have a private party here? Yes!*

We love saying yes!

- *Can you come to my house and cater my private party? Yes!*

- *Can we buy a gift certificate? Yes!*

- *Can we have a donation? Yes!*

- *Is the art for sale? Yes!*

40

- *Can I play your baby grand piano? Yes!*

- *Can you make us a reservation at Café des Amis? Mais, oui!*

You didn't know Don speaks French?

- *Can we sit outside? Yes!*

- *Can we order some food? Yes!*

- *Can we get married at the shoppe like you and Don did? Yes!*

- *Can we become WBJ® club members? Yes!*

- *Can I apply to join the WBJ® team? Yes!*

- *Can I pet the cat? Most definitely Yes!*

- *Can I carry your backpack on your next trip? Yes! (But there's a waiting list.)*

Want to know how we did all that?

By paying attention, asking questions, and listening!

We didn't have every one of those offerings right out of the gate at Wines by Jennifer®. But I learned long ago our customers will tell us everything we need to know if we just let them.

The Wines by Jennifer® Story

I've been to too many businesses where I feel like a transaction, not a guest. I, on the other hand, have always viewed customers not as a transaction opportunity, but instead as a *relationship* opportunity.

And by building relationships, we've built a business. A business based on family, on community, on caring.

We know our customers' names, we know their families, we know their stories.

We know their kids' names, how many dogs they have, where they went on vacation.

We know what they were making for dinner to go with the bottle of wine they bought last night.

Why do we know these things? Because we care about them as *people*!

Does it make for good business? Of course.

But even better, it makes for good friends.

We've seen a lot over the course of almost 18 years in business. We've seen families change, grow, evolve, and yes, unfortunately, sometimes dissolve.

It's life.

But we've also seen couples that met at the shoppe that now have kids in high school.

Couples that got married at the shoppe that return at that same time every year, like swallows to Capistrano, to renew and reminisce.

People that have met in our Tasting Room that now take family vacations together.

The point of all this is not to brag, but to illustrate how the customer loyalty that our approach creates sustains the business. And more importantly, how it sustains us.

We have dozens of people who joined our club on the day we opened nearly two decades ago that are still members today. Almost 18 years of seeing Wines by Jennifer® show up on their credit card statement month after month – amazing!

Don knows this better than anyone, because he still delivers their wines to them every month, a lifetime benefit promised to these legacy club members all those years ago.

The Wines by Jennifer® Story

One of my favorite stories about our customers' loyalty involves a rare unfavorable review on social media we received a couple years ago. It didn't bother us much (harking back to the "can't be all things to all people" thing), but before I knew it, our customers had already sprung to our defense and were flaming the offending complainer right back.

I must admit it was gratifying to see.

I'll end with more from Doug Frost, who commented when asked about Wines by Jennifer® in a recent interview, "To succeed in the wine business, you need to create a loyal base of raving fans like Jennifer has done. It's remarkable, and what really makes them stand out so much. It's just great to see them succeed."

He concluded by saying, "I'm not entirely sure how they make it work, but they sure do."

Thanks for the kind words, Doug.

Maybe it just comes from the service in our bones.

6 Innovators

"We invent faster than they can copy." - Ray Kroc

That quote from the founder of McDonald's has a lot more meaning to me now than it did before I opened Wines by Jennifer® in 2003. Because, like McDonald's, we've had our share of imitators and copycats over the years.

We have always had curiosity seekers at the shoppe, and that's great. But sometimes it was shocking how blatant people could be. Notepads, cameras, barely camouflaged questions, it was borderline ridiculous.

On more than one occasion, I was informed outright that the person in question was going to take our exact concept and open one just like it in Paducah, Peoria, or (insert name of random backwater town here).

I always smiled and wished them luck.

And I meant it, because in my opinion, there's plenty of abundance to go around. If people are drinking wine and having fun somewhere, I'm happy. The way I see it is they'll eventually do it at Wines by Jennifer®, too.

Imitation is the sincerest form of flattery, as they say, so I chose to be flattered.

But, like competitors, we don't particularly concern ourselves with imitators. As always, we focus on serving our customers, and everything else takes care of itself.

So we innovate not out of necessity, but because it's more of a compulsion.

The fact of the matter is that Don and I both have fertile imaginations. It's a condition we purposefully cultivate by consistently applying focused and concentrated thought upon our desired outcome.

As a result, new ideas are rarely a problem.

Execution, on the other hand…

It's not that we're *poor* executors, it's just a matter of having *so much* to execute.

The entrepreneurial paradox, I call it. Oftentimes, there are simply more ideas than resources.

Thankfully, we have a great team of implementers who are also sometimes innovators in their own right – our WBJ® team.

Many of the best ideas we have had at Wines by Jennifer® have come not from us, but from our team.

That's what happens when you surround yourself with the best.

A perfect example is the recent roll-out of our luxury tasting program, a "step-up" product from our regular wine tastings. Available by the ounce or the glass, these ultra-premium wines have been such a huge success that I can't believe we hadn't done it before now.

And it was developed proactively by two of our team members who saw a gap in our offerings and took it upon themselves to fill it.

Brilliant!

That's not to say Don and I haven't had an idea or two along the way. When you've been in business for nearly 18 years, keeping things fresh is always important.

The Wines by Jennifer® Story

Maybe my favorite innovation came along very early, in January of 2005.

For those of you not familiar, the Kansas City area has what could reasonably be described as an obsession with college basketball. Being hockey fans ourselves, it isn't something we pay much attention to, but we certainly respect that others do.

Anyway, there's this little thing in the spring every year called March Madness. You may have heard of it.

Because we opened in April of 2003, it wasn't until March Madness rolled around in 2004 that we got our first taste of what its impact would be on us, considering we are not exactly a sports bar kind of place.

Well, it got a little quiet at the shoppe. Not dead or anything, mind you, but quieter than normal.

Over some wine with our shoppe cat, Pinot, one snowy January Sunday evening in 2005, discussion turned to the upcoming tournament and the slowdown we had experienced the previous year.

Not content to sit idly by and watch this happen again, we decided if you can't beat 'em, join 'em!

Then we got to work.

Like many things Don and I have created, just whose idea this was is the subject of ongoing debate. Usually, in the interest of keeping peace in the family, I just defer to his male ego and let him have the credit.

Even if I really know better.

Anyway, we started to brainstorm, and the wine continued to flow, and the next thing you know, the framework of our own tournament was beginning to come into focus.

To keep the attorneys happy, we would call our creation Wines by Jennifer's Wine March Madness™.

What we came up with looked something like this:

- Our Tasting Room would be the site of one regional per week for the tourney's first three weeks, running concurrent with that "other" tournament.

    - Week One would be the "Americas" Regional with wines from North and South America.

    - Week Two would be the "Euro" Regional with, naturally, European wines.

    - Week Three would be the "Down Under" Regional with wines from Australia, New Zealand, and South Africa.

- Two wines (one white and one red) would advance from each regional based on most sales that week.

- The six advancing wines from the three regionals would then make up our "Surviving Six," held the week of the Final Four.

- The top seller of the Surviving Six would then become our winner-take-all "Champion Wine," to be poured by the glass for the next year.

- Each paid tasting would entitle the taster to submit one "bracket" with picks on which wines they thought would advance. (Those brackets double as a great customer list-builder for us, too!)

- The person with the most correct picks of advancing wines from all four weeks would be the Gold Medalist and win a bottle of each of the Surviving Six wines.

- The Silver Medalist would win a bottle of their favorite red and favorite white from the Surviving Six.

- The Bronze Medalist would win a bottle of their favorite wine from the Surviving Six.

- First tie-breaker would be awarded to those with the most brackets entered.

- Second tie-breaker would be awarded to those picking the Champion Wine.

- Third tie-breaker would be random drawing.

Like everything else we do, the tournament was constructed with a specific goal in mind. That goal, of course, was to promote wine sales!

Little did we know what was in store.

Like a little snowball rolling down a mountain, the tournament started modestly in the first year or two. Everyone agreed it was a fun idea, but it was more casual back in those days.

The winners had modest win totals, and people were treating it more as a novelty than anything else.

But this little snowball gained momentum, slowly at first, then accelerating until it started to look more like an avalanche coming down the mountain.

Our little "novelty" had begun to take on a life of its own.

The electricity in the air every year in the spring as the event approached was palpable. People were filled with excitement, anticipation, and energy, because really, who doesn't love a good competition?

"What wines are competing this year?"

"What countries are represented this year?"

"Is the defending champ coming back?"

"When's the bracket coming out?"

And the eminently transparent one, *"So, Jennifer, which wine do <u>you</u> think will win this year?"*

Yeah, right.

Then even the wineries started getting involved!

One of our regular participants, South Africa's Backsberg Estate Cellars, began producing and distributing their own Wines by Jennifer's Wine March Madness™ videos to drum up support and issue friendly challenges to their fellow Down Under competitors.

It was great to see!

Probably best of all, a hard-core group of contestants began to emerge.

This very eclectic group of competitors seemingly had only one thing in common: they all wanted to beat the living daylights out of all the others!

Always seeking an edge, they began exhibiting some, shall we say, "obsessive" behavior in varying degrees.

We had people "dumpster diving" in our recycle bin looking for empty bottles to calculate just how many bottles of each wine had been poured, clearly oblivious to the fact that many other full bottles of those wines went out the door to good homes!

We had to hide the master party schedule we keep in the kitchen because people kept sneaking peeks to estimate what kind of effect our parties might have had on sales.

We witnessed contestants sitting down to do their tasting, only to be joined by one or more of the other die-hards. Then, it became *mano a mano*, a sort of "dueling tastings " scenario, each one waiting for the other to blink, each one vying to be the last man (or woman) standing.

People were doing two, three, four tastings at a time, sometimes consecutively, sometimes concurrently, sometimes both.

And coming back daily to wash/rinse/repeat!

Because the winner would be the wine that sold the most, we had customers secretly returning to make wine purchases and influence the outcome in favor of their choice without being detected.

And that was just one-half of a husband-wife team bound and determined not to lose to his/her (*protects identity*) spouse.

It got to the point that I thought they all were going to demand I put up a "Wines by Jennifer's Wine March Madness™ Cam" in the Tasting Room so they could have real-time surveillance on their opponents' activities.

Needless to say, the bar had been raised and the amount of commitment to even remotely be in the conversation for winning had become significantly elevated.

It was like the wine version of a Cold War arms race.

We even began working around peoples' absences for work or vacation. We would pour them take-home tastings with brackets to complete and they would return the glasses with their brackets when they got back from wherever it was they were going.

Everyone knew that missing time during the tournament would be crippling to their chances of winning.

We had all kinds of wild outcomes: the need to measure specific bottle fill levels side-by-side to determine winners, wines that tied forcing "overtime," going to tiebreakers to determine the Gold Medalist, you name it, we probably saw it.

Not to mention the tallying of the brackets at the end of the tournament.

There were hundreds! I thought I was going to have to retain Price-Waterhouse to assist in the process.

The awards ceremony evolved, too.

Initially, we just made a trophy and presented it to the winner while awarding their prizes.

Then we added a "net cutting" ceremony of sorts, where we would adorn the champ with a basketball net and shoot some videos of them being crowned.

Then, in recognition of the commitment required to compete, we started having parties for those in the running, complete with food, wine, and formal coronations.

We even had a magnum that we had polished off at the first coronation party that became a traveling trophy. The medalists would all sign it, and it would go home with the Gold Medalist on the condition that it be returned next year to be passed on to the next winner, a la the Stanley Cup.

Ironically, what had been a slight lull in the calendar had now become one of our busiest times of the year.

We had created a monster!

It was exciting and fun and profitable, and it still is.

I just love it when a plan comes together.

Our annual Oktoberfest celebration had its roots as a public anniversary celebration, held for the first time in April, 2004, one year after our grand opening. In true "fest" style, it featured outsized amounts of food and wine poured over a several hour period throughout the entire shoppe.

Like our Wines by Jennifer's Wine March Madness™, it has also become an arms race over the years, with the different wine selections now routinely totaling more than 100.

The event, however, had begun to be plagued by poor weather and overcrowding.

So again, by paying attention, asking questions, and listening to our customers, we modified and improved it. We changed the date, privatized access to our club members and their guests only, and moved the location to our beautiful, grapevine-canopied Wine Garden.

Now, this finely tuned machine is our most highly anticipated event of the year.

The true innovation, however, came when we began to invite the participation of winemakers we had met through our travels, first from around the country, then from around the world.

And if attendance and wine sales are the measuring sticks, the very first international winemaker we ever hosted made the biggest splash of all.

It would not be a stretch to call Kevin Judd New Zealand winemaking royalty. The founding winemaker at Cloudy Bay, where he remained for their first 25 vintages, Kevin established his own small, family-owned winery, Greywacke, in Marlborough in 2009.

We had met Kevin on our first trip to New Zealand in 2014, when, in his words, "Don and Jennifer just rolled up one day."

(Isn't "just rolling up" what everyone does when they visit New Zealand wine country?)

Born in England and raised in Adelaide, South Australia, we immediately felt a kinship when he told us that, like us, he did not "grow up under a vine."

Kevin only produces seven wines, all well recognized, highly regarded, and extremely delicious, I can assure you.

Not only that, he is also one of New Zealand's finest wine photographers, as the labels on all his wine bottles will attest.

As our visit concluded, we thanked him for his time, his wines, and the beautiful book of his New Zealand vineyard photography he gave us, and we moved on to our next stop.

Several months later, Don got wind that Kevin was in America promoting his wines. He immediately got on the phone with the Greywacke importer, with whom we had a good relationship from carrying the Greywacke wines at Wines by Jennifer®.

Don inquired about Kevin's itinerary, and, not surprisingly, learned that "flyover" country here in the Midwest was not on it.

But Don had an ace in the hole.

What if we made Kevin the headliner for our upcoming 2015 Oktoberfest, which, thanks to a marketing piece Don still considers one of his finest, was shaping up to be the most highly attended in our history?

Well, let's just say "flyover" country just became "stopover" country.

We were absolutely thrilled to have the chance to welcome Kevin, his wife Kimberley, and his marketing chief Richard Ellis to Parkville.

We were even more thrilled when, after we gave the Greywacke team a tour of the shoppe, Kevin said to us, "This is quite a complex operation. I've never seen anything quite like it. It's like being in somebody's home."

Very flattering indeed, especially when considering the source.

After kicking off the day with a private brunch for our A-list customers, our Kiwi guests then proceeded to knock it out of the park at Oktoberfest, not surprising given their wines and their charm.

One innovation Don and I are quite proud of is what we dubbed our WBJ® Virtual Tasting series. The launch event took place at Toad Hollow Vineyards in 2011 in Healdsburg, California.

Toad Hollow was founded in 1993 in Sonoma County by Todd (Dr. Toad) Williams (brother of comedian Robin Williams) and his business partner, the late pioneering Sonoma winemaker Rodney Strong.

Having met Todd at trade tasting events in the past, we were fond of him and his wine, and were sorry to learn of his passing in 2007.

But Todd's widow Frankie is a ball of fire who is still going strong, and when we approached her with our idea, she bought in immediately.

The basic concept of our WBJ® Virtual Tasting series was that Don and I would visit wineries and taste wines on location with the owner and/or winemaker, while simultaneously engaging with our customers back at Wines by Jennifer® in Parkville via Skype and a big-screen TV.

The customers at the shoppe would be tasting the same wines we were tasting right along with us, hence the "Virtual Tasting" moniker. As an added twist, we also had a few remote participants who were given access to the broadcast by purchasing Toad Hollow wine at our shoppe in advance.

After some quick coordination between their techies and ours, we were all set to go live.

The event was great and went off without a hitch. We had fun, made friends, sold wine, made our customers happy, and then…well, imitation is the sincerest form of flattery.

We went on to do other WBJ® Virtual Tastings both abroad and in Parkville, but we'll always have a soft spot in our hearts for Frankie, Toad Hollow, and our very first WBJ® Virtual Tasting.

7 We're Working!

"We're working!" is a phrase Don and I began to use anytime we stumbled on a great idea or were involved in a fun activity somewhere that we knew could apply to our business.

It originated on a family vacation in 2007 that included a side trip to the Finger Lakes wine region in New York State, much to Daniel's dismay. At the age of 13, he was still too young to appreciate a good wine country experience.

After what was, in his opinion, one too many winery stops, the "wining" from the back seat was in full swing.

Finally, I'd heard enough. I turned around, looked him in the eye, and said sternly and in all seriousness, *"Young man, your mother is working!"*

Don gave me one of his patented "you must be joking" looks, and we both started laughing, knowing full well a new phrase had just been coined.

We're Working!

It's now our long-standing inside joke used only partially in jest, because we understand full well our work is usually considered everyone else's play.

For example:

- Discover a wine purse in South Africa that we can import and sell at the shoppe?

  We're working!

- Find a great wine in Romania we can use for our club?

  We're working!

- See a wine garden in Burgundy covered in vines and realize we can do the same thing back home at WBJ®?

  We're working!

- Travel to professional wine tastings around the world looking for the best wines for our shoppe?

  We're working!

- Cover ourselves in cozy blankets at a restaurant on the shores of Lake Geneva and realize they would be perfect on the front porch of the shoppe in the fall?

  We're working!

- Help judge the 700+ wines entered each year in the Jefferson Cup wine competition?

  We're really working!

The list goes on and on.

Even when we splurge in our travels, as we do from time to time, I really feel like we're working. That's because I truly believe that in order to deliver a *luxury experience*, as we strive to do at Wines by Jennifer®, you have to actually *experience luxury.*

Virtually everything we do is evaluated through the prism of "how can we take this and apply it to our business?"

It's just our nature, and honestly, it's hard to turn off.

It's a mindset that stems from something marketing genius Marty Edelston taught. He believed that, viewed properly, every situation is a learning opportunity.

That's exactly how our nationally recognized beer program got started.

In 2004, we were "working" our way through Belgium, the Netherlands, and Luxembourg (an area known collectively as "Benelux") on our way to France.

If you know anything about those countries, you know it's more about the beer than anything else.

We're Working!

Being subscribers to the "when in Rome" school of thought, we were faithfully drinking our share of beer.

One night at about 2am on the patio of the hotel (24/7 bar – Ibis for the win!) where we were staying in Antwerp, it hit us:

"These Belgian beers are fantastic. We love beer. Why in the world are we not offering beer?"

Bam!

We're working!

The WBJ® beer program has since mushroomed into something we never imagined all those years ago.

Our timing for introducing the program could not have been better. We preceded the craft beer explosion by several years, then rode the wave when it hit.

In fact, in recognition of the quality and scope of our program, Don was invited to be a member of a small, select panel of experts that provides beer reviews for a national trade publication.

Besides Don, we also have two home brewers on our WBJ® team, which means there is always someone ready, willing, and able to discuss all things beer.

And one of our long-time club members, Tony DiPlacito, actually completed part of his Cicerone®

(think: beer sommelier) training at a special WBJ®
Trappist BeerFest event we held a few years ago.

Since then, Tony has leveraged his own success as a
home brewer to launch a brand new brewery, Wind
Shift Brewing, in Blue Springs, Missouri.

So, yeah, the name may be *Wines* by Jennifer®, but I
like to think we also know a little about beer.

Spirits, too, for that matter.

We began our spirits program not long after we
introduced beer, but we presented it in a completely
different way.

Don has long been a fan of whisk(e)y, particularly
Scotch, dating even back to his college days when most
of his friends were drinking watered-down beer.

Over time, he began to notice what seemed to be a
growing interest in whiskey from conversations he had
with customers in our Tasting Room.

One day, he came to me with the idea of doing a special
event on Scotch. He knew Scotland well from having
visited; he knew the distillation process from studying
it; and he certainly knew good Scotch from bad from
drinking it!

"Why not?" I thought, and suggested that we also include food pairings to go with the Scotch and the educational experience he would provide.

So we got busy with our preparations, and began to sell the event.

The response surprised even Don.

Once word got out what we had planned, the phone started ringing and it never stopped. Even after the event quickly sold out, we continued to get calls and inquiries from customers wanting in.

We were on to something!

Demand was high, and as always, we're going to give the customers what they want.

So we scheduled another.

And another—which we immediately sold out to one person with one phone call. All 22 seats gone, just like that!

This customer had effectively just scheduled his very own private Scotch tasting party at Wines by Jennifer®.

I think we began to see the handwriting on the wall, though, when we scheduled two events in back-to-back weeks. The seats were all gone almost before the ink was dry on our special events calendar.

What we were doing, while highly successful, was clearly not scalable.

Some time later, on a trip to Tokyo to visit our friends, the Miuras, whom you'll meet later, we were introduced to the Japanese whisky culture.

It was fascinating to observe. Picture an insatiable appetite for luxury and prestige, and an equally unlimited willingness to spend for it, and you'd have a pretty good idea.

A visit to one of the whisky bars that line the streets of Tokyo provided the inspiration. It was there that we saw ultra-premium whiskies with elaborate presentations being devoured by Japanese businessmen, and that's when the light bulb went off.

We would just convert from a special event model to an on-demand model with an ultra-premium focus.

Since then, our on-demand spirits menu has expanded to include numerous other categories of spirits and liqueurs both clear and dark, all welcomed with open arms by our thirsty customers.

Because, *we're working!*

Part Three

HERE TO STAY

8 We've Arrived

Don and I have always been very confident people, and by extension, we were always very confident in the success of Wines by Jennifer®. There have been, however, several of what I call "aha" moments along the way. These random examples of our growing exposure and reach gave us even more confidence that we had achieved the traction necessary for a thriving and sustainable business.

It was shortly after opening Wines by Jennifer® in the spring of 2003 that I received a phone call from one of the wine distributors with whom I worked. She mentioned that she had a wine producer with her that she was escorting to select accounts around the city, and asked if I would be available for them to visit and taste their wine together.

Nothing unusual about that. Nothing unusual, that is, until she told me the producer's name.

It was none other than Dick Vermeil.

Although Dick was more famous as the head coach of the Kansas City Chiefs, he had deep wine roots as well. Born and raised in California's Napa Valley, Dick had begun a hobby winery in his hometown of Calistoga in 1999.

Would I be available to taste his very first release, the 2002 vintage, with them?

Why yes, I think I might be able to work that in!

As a long-time Chiefs fan and season ticket holder, I was more than a little excited to host Coach Vermeil. Any anxiety I might have had, though, immediately faded away upon meeting him.

Despite his celebrity, Dick was extremely pleasant and down-to-earth. He had a special way of making you feel at ease, as if you had been friends forever.

They were accompanied by Dick's winemaker, Paul Smith, highly acclaimed in his own right for his previous work at Robert Mondavi and Opus One in Napa.

After sampling through the wines (all excellent) and giving Dick and Paul a tour of the shoppe, Paul insisted that Dick and I pose for a picture together. He was an avid photographer.

Twist my arm!

To this day, I still proudly display that picture in my office at the shoppe, but it was its placement elsewhere that delighted me the most.

Former Chiefs defensive lineman Ken "Fuzzy" Kremer and his wife Lisa are friends and long-time supporters of the shoppe. They happened to be visiting Napa Valley later that summer and had just left Dick and Paul's tasting room, when Lisa called the shoppe.

"Jennifer, did you know there's a picture of you and Dick Vermeil hanging in his tasting room?"

Wow, I did not, but how cool is that?!

I continued to get random reports from other customers that had visited the Calistoga tasting room and noticed that picture, and hearing about it always brought a smile to my face.

But that's not the only fun story related to Dick's visit to Wines by Jennifer®.

During the exciting 2003 season when the Chiefs finished 13-3, kicker Morten Andersen was lining up for a game-winning field goal against the arch-rival Oakland Raiders.

Coach Vermeil knew Andersen was a big wine guy, and tried to relax him before the critical kick by offering him a bottle of Bryant Family Vineyards Cabernet, a rare and valuable Napa "cult" wine, from his personal cellar if he made it.

Andersen did indeed make the crucial kick to win the game, but when news of the incentive leaked, the No Fun League nixed it as a violation of the salary cap.

Conveniently enough, it just so happened that I had purchased every single bottle available to the state of Missouri of the 2000 vintage Bryant, and still had one for sale at Wines by Jennifer®. Somehow, the local media got wind of that, and it was on.

Television crews flocked to the shoppe, interviewing me and getting footage of the infamous Bryant Cab on display at Wines by Jennifer®.

It was like I had a unicorn or something.

After a couple days of welcome media attention, a steady stream of Chiefs players and other media personalities began visiting the shoppe, curious to see what all the hype was about.

Even Morten himself showed up one day to see what he had missed out on.

I decided then and there to never sell that bottle, instead keeping it for myself as a souvenir of those exciting days.

And I also decided long ago the only way that special bottle of 2000 Bryant Family Vineyards Cabernet Sauvignon would ever get opened and shared would be at a reunion of the protagonists of the story.

Dick?

Morten?

Fuzzy?

The Bryant and I are ready.

Another big "aha" moment occurred when Wines by Jennifer® was in its fourth year of operation, in the fall of 2006.

Don and I were on a two-week West Coast wine trip, beginning in Oregon and slowly winding our way southward down the coast. The San Francisco Bay Area was our final destination, where we were going to rendezvous with some California-based friends and our son Daniel, who would be flying in from Kansas City.

On our way south, we passed through both Mendocino and Lake Counties in northern California, excellent yet underappreciated wine regions overshadowed by their respective neighbors to the south, Sonoma and Napa.

Back in Parkville, we had a charter club member-turned-friend named Alan Mauch, sadly now deceased, who had been telling us for some time about a winery he was helping get started in Lake County called Six Sigma. Alan had worked with the founder of the winery, a Dane by the name of Kaj Ahlmann, for the re-insurance arm of General Electric in Kansas City.

As Alan described it, Kaj had spearheaded the implementation of Six Sigma methods for Jack Welch at GE, and he was so committed to its "never-ending improvement" philosophy that he decided to name his winery after it. He was positioning Six Sigma as a customer-driven, "experiential" winery featuring ranch-grown food and estate wines sourced from the 4300-acre ranch he had purchased specifically for that purpose.

We were definitely intrigued to see the winery and meet Kaj, since we had built Wines by Jennifer® based upon those very same experiential, customer-focused, constant improvement principles, minus the 4300 acres, of course!

In the meantime, trusting Alan's considerable expertise in the subject (he had a hobby vineyard and an excellent palate), we began to carry a few Six Sigma wines at Wines by Jennifer®.

As we climbed the Mayacamas Mountains that separate Mendocino and Lake Counties (as they do Sonoma and Napa Counties to the south), we paused at the crest to admire the stunning views of Clear Lake down below. While enjoying the scenery, I was somehow suddenly compelled to call Kaj.

Alan had given us Kaj's business card with the instructions to check in if we were ever in the area. He had told Kaj all about us, and informed us that he would be happy to take our call.

Well, we're right here, so no time like the present, I thought, invoking yet again our standard travel operating procedure of spontaneity.

To my utter amazement, Kaj picked up. "Hello, this is Kaj," he said in his formal Danish accent.

"Hello, Kaj, this is Jennifer from Wines by Jennifer®. I'm from Kansas City and Alan Mauch is a mutual friend…," I began, before Kaj interrupted.

"Yes, Jennifer, I know all about you. In fact, I was just talking about you on the airplane today."

Whaaaaaat?

Kaj had been returning from Bermuda earlier that day, where he had spent time attending to business in one of the myriad high-powered roles he occupied in the re-insurance world. While on a connecting flight to Atlanta, he was seated next to a lady going home, and somehow the discovery was made that they had something in common: each had formerly lived in the Kansas City area.

One thing led to another, and eventually the conversation turned to wine. (Yay!) As Kaj recounted it, the first thing the lady asked was if he had been to Wines by Jennifer® in Parkville.

Kaj replied that, no, he hadn't been nor had he met me, but that he heard good things and that we sold his wine.

Talk about coincidence!

Kaj had just landed in Sacramento and was heading home to the ranch. He suggested we meet him there later that day and he would show us around.

Deal!

We arrived at the ranch at the appointed hour, punched in the code Kaj had given us for the gate, and began to drive to the ranch house.

And we drove. And we drove. And we drove.

You can't necessarily appreciate the massiveness of 4300 acres until you begin to see it for yourself. Imagine Central Park in New York times five, and you'd be in the ballpark.

Finally, after about 25 minutes from the time we entered the gate, we arrived at a very modest structure that had a couple of lights on and an old farm pickup truck in the driveway.

Surely this couldn't be the winery, could it?

As we got closer, we noticed the license plate on the truck: Johnson County, Kansas.

Paydirt!

Being the busy man that he was, Kaj hadn't quite gotten around to changing the tags after his move from Johnson County, Kansas to Lake County, California.

There was too much excellent wine to be made!

We knocked on the door, and it was opened by none other than Kaj himself.

He greeted us each with a glass of wine and we began a brief tour of what was serving as a temporary winery until the beautiful, brand-spanking-new Six Sigma winery being built nearby was finished.

Once the tour was complete, the pouring then began in earnest.

A more modest, welcoming, and friendly man you'd be hard-pressed to find. Despite a long list of impressive credentials, our conversation revealed that Kaj was really just a simple farmer at heart. It was a lifestyle he had inherited from his grandfather, who had been a farmer back in Denmark.

As he put it, he had gone from "who's who" to "who's he," an acknowledgment that despite his extensive resume, as a winegrower, he was basically a novice.

But like any person of accomplishment, you find the holes in that resume and you fill them. Kaj chose to do this by enrolling in what is probably the most prestigious oenology school in America, University of California-Davis, where he completed his viticultural studies just in time for his first harvest in 2005.

So like a proud parent, over the course of the evening, he tasted us through that entire first vintage while giving us the fascinating backstory of Six Sigma.

We've Arrived

Many of the wines we were familiar with from having them on the shelves at Wines by Jennifer®, but we were certainly happy to re-visit them, especially when poured by the man responsible for them in the first place!

After a long but thoroughly enjoyable evening, we all agreed it was about time to call it a night. Kaj asked about our plans for a place to stay, and we admitted to him that we had none. In his charmingly hospitable way, he insisted we stay in a spare bedroom he had at the ranch, given the late hour and the empty wine bottles strewn around us.

We gratefully accepted his generous offer, and that's how we came to spend the night at Six Sigma Ranch in the bunkbeds of Kaj Ahlmann's kids, nodding off to sleep secure in the knowledge that we had just added another priceless story to our growing repertoire.

Way back in the fall of 2002, buried in the middle of all the seemingly endless preparations necessary for opening the business, one day Don and I looked around and asked ourselves if it might be convenient to actually have, you know, a name for it? Like, something a little more creative than what we had been calling it to that point: "The Shoppe." Several brainstorming sessions had already been conducted, usually fueled by wine, but so far nothing had resonated.

Then one day, almost out of the blue, Don asked me, "What do you think about Wines by Jennifer?"

Ding, ding, ding, ding. We have a winner!

Including my name in the name of the business has turned out to be what Don refers to as his "accidental stroke of genius." It has no doubt contributed significantly to the quasi-celebrity status I seem to have achieved.

If I had a dollar for every time I heard:

"Is there really a Jennifer?"

Or, "I wanna be Jennifer!"

Or, "Are you THE Jennifer?"

While humbling and flattering for sure, it happens frequently enough that I tease Don that I'm going to have my name tag changed from "Jennifer" to "THE Jennifer."

We even routinely have Jennifers (or someone who knows a Jennifer) arriving from random locations, completing their pilgrimage to the shoppe so they can buy a glass with "their" name on it – which we always insist they accept with our compliments and gratitude.

And it's all Don's fault.

This phenomenon is not just confined to Kansas City, either.

Our Wines by Jennifer®-branded wine glasses have been spotted all over the country. I guess being in business since 2003 and having loyal club members in nearly 30 states will do that.

We even had someone report that they were visiting friends in London once, when, much to their amazement, they opened up the bar to see Wines by Jennifer® glasses sitting inside begging to be filled!

Finally, there was the time when, upon returning home from a meeting with our corporate attorney in Las Vegas, I was told by one of our club members that a friend of theirs thought they recognized me in the Vegas airport and asked them if it could've been "THE Jennifer."

I think that was the day when we really realized "We've Arrived."

9 Ichiro & Emiko

Of all the things we do at Wines by Jennifer®, by far the most gratifying and rewarding are the relationships we form and the differences we are able to make in our customers' lives. No story better exemplifies this than the one you are about to hear: the story of our Japanese friends, Ichiro and Emiko Miura.

Like meteors in the sky, Ichiro and Emiko flashed into, across, and ultimately out of our world in what looking back seems like an instant. But, also like a meteor, they left an indelible impression that will last a lifetime.

The Miuras first came to us as customers in mid-2011, shortly after arriving in Kansas City for Ichiro's latest business assignment. Although they never said as much, I'm sure Kansas City was considerably less glamorous than the two previous temporary assignments they had just completed in Italy and Germany.

And so it began, just like clockwork for the next year and a half. Precisely at noon every other Saturday,

Ichiro and Emiko would appear on our doorstep for their biweekly wine excursion to downtown Parkville from their home on the Plaza.

Despite the considerable gaps between us in language and culture, we quickly identified a shared appreciation and love of the finer things in life, namely food, wine, and travel. Communication was difficult, but lots of smiling, nodding, and the occasional *kampai* went a long way as we built a bond of friendship over the next several months.

Fun memories of them both cross my mind often, such as Emiko's love of our reigning Wines by Jennifer's Wine March Madness™ Champion, an Australian Riesling that always seemed to find a way into her glass whether she asked for it or not.

We even had a fun, little "inside joke" we all liked to share together. As avid travelers, when our conversations turned to places visited, as it often did, none of us ever answered "no" to the question, "Have you been there?"

It was always, "Not yet!"

So it seemed like business as usual when the Miuras arrived on a bright sunny Saturday, right on schedule at noon sharp, in mid-December, 2012. We were soon to find out, however, it was anything but.

The Wines by Jennifer® Story

Don and I had come to the shoppe early that day, busily making preparations for our annual Wines by Jennifer® Luxury Holiday Open House being held later that evening. When Ichiro and Emiko arrived, they seemed unusually reserved, but we didn't really think much of it at the time because Japanese tend to be pretty private people in general.

Reverting to form, they made their way to our Tasting Room and tasted through the wines on the table. They then picked up their wine carriers and made their usual beeline straight upstairs to the France and Italy rooms to stock up on their wine inventory.

But the fact that this day was different became even more apparent when, upon checkout, their usual case purchase had dwindled to just a couple of bottles. My suspicions were confirmed when Emiko discreetly took me aside and said that sadly this would be their last visit to Wines by Jennifer®. As it turned out, unspecified family considerations required that they leave Kansas City immediately and return home to Tokyo.

It was a very humbling moment indeed when Emiko shared with me that of all their time spent in Kansas City, the very best memory they would take with them back home to Japan was the time they spent with us at Wines by Jennifer®. And as a token of their appreciation, they wanted to present us with a very special (and valuable) gift: a 1985 Domaine Simon Bize *Marc de Bourgogne* from their personal collection.

If you're not familiar, Simon Bize is arguably the finest producer in the Burgundy sub-region of Savigny-lès-Beaune, an appellation we have personally visited and enjoyed (partially for the wine, partially because it is also home to an amazing military jet boneyard). It just so happened that Ichiro and Emiko had a personal connection with the winery because the proprietor, Patrick Bize (since deceased), had a Japanese wife with whom they were friends.

Respect for their privacy (not to mention a building of emotion) prevented me from asking about the reason for their sudden departure. But as a gesture of appreciation for what they had meant to us, both personally and professionally, before they could leave, Don immediately whisked them downstairs for a private tasting of the wines and spirits we would be pouring for our Open House guests later that evening.

Don would later share with me the sheer delight on Ichiro's face when he saw a 1999 Bertani Amarone we had pulled from our personal cellar featured in the lineup. As the wine connoisseur he was, Ichiro certainly understood and appreciated what he was about to enjoy. As a matter of fact, knowing him as we did, it wouldn't have surprised us at all if Ichiro was a personal friend of the Bertani winemaker.

Although we had assured them we would meet again one day, the look on their faces as they left Parkville one final time is as clear in my mind today as it was back then. I still remember Emiko pausing on the sidewalk as they approached their car, pausing to take a last look at what she called her "special place." It was a mixture of sadness and uncertainty that is difficult to describe.

Fast forward several months, to the fall of 2013. Don and I were preparing for one of our patented around-the-world excursions thanks to another one of his "travel game" projects (more on that later). On this occasion, it happened to include a 23-hour connection in Tokyo, and we both knew immediately what that meant – the perfect opportunity to re-connect with our Japanese friends!

We were able to coordinate our reunion via back-and-forth email correspondence with Emiko, and so it was with excitement and a plan that we landed at Toyko's Narita Airport on December 3, 2013. After a long year of separation, it was time for the reunion.

Our flight from Seoul's Incheon Airport to Narita thankfully arrived on time, and we began the lengthy 70-minute train ride from the airport to our hotel near the Tokyo Dome. The plan was for Ichiro and Emiko to meet us in the hotel lobby there and escort us to one of their favorite restaurants for a fun evening enjoying Japanese food and wine culture with our friends.

After freshening up and preparing for the evening, Don and I made our way to the hotel lobby with anticipation and excitement, both of which were immediately drained when we saw our friends.

Weak and emaciated, with a stocking cap covering what was obviously a hairless head, the reason for the Miuras' sudden departure from Kansas City back to Tokyo was immediately clear – Ichiro was dying.

Drawing upon every ounce of strength we had, Don and I tried desperately to keep our composure for everybody's sake, and were amazingly able to hold our emotions together throughout the evening.

Despite his illness, Ichiro took great pride in directing the entire evening's menu and agenda. He orchestrated it in his usual expert fashion, despite the fact that he could barely enjoy it due to his condition. It was a demonstration of dignity and grace that I will never forget.

At the end of the evening, Ichiro and Emiko escorted us to our cab, where we all exchanged hugs in the streets of Tokyo. The emotion behind Ichiro's long embrace, combined with his obvious physical frailty, left little doubt that this would be the last time we would ever see our Japanese friend.

Less than two weeks after returning home, we received the sad but not unexpected news via email from Emiko that Ichiro was gone, taken by esophagus cancer. It was a sad and cruel irony that one of the things he lived for the most, enjoyment of fine food and wine, is one of the things that had been compromised the most during his long struggle.

Emiko also made a point in her email to express her heartfelt thanks for our visit. It was her firm belief, she said, that the anticipation of seeing us one more time had extended Ichiro's life.

Don and I immediately went to work making arrangements for the next week's theme in our Tasting Room to be "A Tribute to Ichiro." The lineup, of course, would be nothing but the best French and Italian wines, just as he would have wanted it.

After sending our condolences, we promised Emiko that we would stay in touch, and we did. So we were very excited to give her the news that another around-the-world excursion we had planned for the fall of 2014 included another 23-hour stop in Tokyo.

This reunion would prove to be quite emotional as well.

Ichiro & Emiko

Our rendezvous took place at one of Emiko's favorite Tokyo restaurants. Once the tears were wiped away, we took our shoes off and sat cross-legged on the floor in a private room to enjoy a traditional Japanese lunch memorable for more than just the obvious reasons.

For one, it was so touching to watch Emiko delight in pulling up her favorite picture of Ichiro on her smartphone and placing it strategically on the table. The symbolism of him being with us in spirit if not body created a memory that is forever etched into my mind.

Another was sharing our mutual enjoyment of the Kansas City Royals as they competed in the 2014 World Series against the San Francisco Giants, an experience enriched by the appearance in the Royals lineup of Japanese outfielder Nori Aoki. We followed along with live updates during lunch for the game taking place "last night," thanks to the 15-hour time difference between Tokyo and Kansas City.

But alas, all too soon, the end of our lunch was upon us. Although we knew the way quite well having just made the trip, Emiko insisted on escorting us back to the train station to catch the Narita Express.

While she claimed it was merely to keep us from getting lost, I choose to believe otherwise.

10 Doing Well by Doing Good

Philanthropy has been an important part of my life for as long as I can remember. Giving and helping others enriches me in countless ways, and provides much needed perspective for the difficult times that everyone occasionally endures.

My volunteer work has benefited me in other, less obvious ways as well. The ability to interact and connect with accomplished, like-minded people while serving others has provided me with many opportunities I would not have had otherwise.

Beginning in my corporate days, and continuing throughout most of my adult life, I have been privileged to serve on the boards of many non-profit organizations, including:

- Ewing Kauffman Greater Kansas City Fund

- Wings Over Mid-America/Angel Flight Central

- Amelia Earhart Birthplace Museum

I have also enjoyed volunteering at these and other organizations over the years. Of the many I have been involved with, mentoring young people through the YouthFriends program and flying Angel Flight mercy missions for people in need have been favorites.

Although I never labeled it as such, this philosophy is one that direct marketing icon Brian Kurtz calls "100/0." The idea is that you always give 100% of yourself with zero expectation of anything in return. Giving for the sake of giving, more or less, with no particular agenda or motive.

It is an approach we have also embraced at Wines by Jennifer®.

It is a fact of life for small businesses to be solicited frequently for donations and contributions to all sorts of causes both large and small.

So one of the most rewarding aspects of our success at Wines by Jennifer® is that it has provided a tremendous platform to continue making these contributions on a regular and consistent basis.

But in the early days, it wasn't so easy. Our response to requests was inconsistent, to put it "charitably."

One donation here, another there, some large, some small. The only constant was that all of them required capital, both mental and physical.

There had to be a better way!

Then it dawned on me.

Why not just donate two free wine tastings with souvenir keepsake Wines by Jennifer® glasses to every organization that asks?

Every. Single. One.

From little Johnny's youth baseball team to the largest 501(c)3, we are now able to give to them all, and it's always the same.

No thought required, no decisions necessary. Easy, peasy, just the way we like it.

As an added bonus, we're often told our donation was the most popular item at the event!

So it's been that way ever since.

Part Four

THE TRAVEL

11 Global Vagabonds

I have always loved to travel. Ever since I started visiting my grandparents in my childhood at their home on Oklahoma's Grand Lake O' the Cherokees, I have long had a strong sense of "wanderlust."

Probably nothing demonstrates this more loudly and clearly than when I decided to take travel matters into my own hands by becoming a pilot in 1997. It was one of the best decisions I ever made, because aviation literally changed my life.

The freedom, the mobility, the sense of accomplishment, the community around which general aviation is built, the challenges both mental and physical, all these factors combined to instill in me a very deep love of flying which I still have today.

And like most things, when I'm in, I'm *all in.*

Not satisfied with just obtaining my private pilot certificate, I immediately began to pursue my instrument rating so that I could fly in adverse weather, providing me more utility and safety.

A commercial certificate, and high-performance, complex, and tailwheel aircraft endorsements all followed in short order, obstacles in my path falling like dominoes.

But I still wasn't satisfied.

Back then, in my mind, I wasn't going to be a real pilot until I owned my own airplane, so guess what came next?

That's right, it wasn't long before I bought my very first airplane, a 1977 Piper Archer II, which I immediately began using for both personal and business purposes.

And because I am constantly seeking new ways to challenge myself, in 1999 I decided to enter the Air Race Classic, an annual race across North America open only to women aviators.

The Air Race Classic is always transcontinental in length, although the origin and destination are not necessarily on the East and West Coasts. The 1999 version began in El Paso, Texas and ended in Cleveland, Ohio, with several intermediate stops along the way, including an international leg across the Canadian border into Toronto.

Before I departed for El Paso, one of the local TV stations interviewed me in front of my airplane in my hangar at Johnson County Executive Airport in Olathe, Kansas. I appreciated the coverage, because now my family and friends could monitor my progress every night on the 10:00 news!

Of the 42 aircraft that started that race, my co-pilot (and former wing walker) Loretta Jones and I were among the 32 that finished. Our results were compromised by a cracked cylinder that developed in my Archer's 4-cylinder Lycoming engine, but it was extremely satisfying just to finish the race.

So although it wasn't originally by design, it is quite convenient that Wines by Jennifer® has given me such a wonderful outlet to continue to scratch that "itch" for travel, one for which Don and I have now become quite well known. It gives purpose, meaning, and intention to our trips, because these days a winery, a brewery, or a distillery (or often all three!) can be found almost anywhere.

We know this to be true because we've seen it first-hand. Tasting local wine in such unexpected places as Alaska, Hawaii, Indonesia, Myanmar, China, Morocco, and Thailand (just to name a few) proved to us over and over that love of the vine is nearly universal.

Frequent travel to all these far-flung places has definitely cemented our reputation as the "wandering wine experts." In fact, that reputation has grown to such heights that rarely does a day pass that I don't hear some variation of "Where are you going?" or "Where have you been?"

Because of the constant interest that was expressed, we began to understand that our customers were living vicariously through our travels. They appreciated that we were out in the field, doing what we used to call in my old agricultural days "ground truthing."

Separating the wheat from the chaff, if you will.

Because we were paying attention to all this interest, it was only a matter of time before we began to incorporate WBJ®-directed tourism into our mix.

And since then, we've done a little bit of everything:

- walking "progressive" wine dinners around downtown Parkville

- open-air trolley "progressive" wine dinners around Kansas City

- weekend caravans to Missouri wine country using various modes of transportation from cars to vans to trains

- open-air "Beer Trolley Tours" to Kansas City-
  area breweries

All that experience came in handy, too, as it prepared us
well for our biggest wine tourism event to date: serving
as wine hosts in 2016 on our very own sold-out Wines
by Jennifer® Danube River Wine Cruise.

Our customers have also benefited from our travels in
many other ways. Unique wine club selections from
obscure places, formal "travelogue" tasting events
themed around our trips, and a steady stream of stories
from our adventures are just a few of the things that
have *them* thanking *us* for being out there "working" on
their behalf.

Travel has benefited *us* in so many other ways, too,
some obvious and some not so obvious. The ability to
travel far and wide multiple times a year, often for
extended periods of time, definitely gives you an
understanding of places you can never get if you don't
personally experience it.

You can taste wine and read about where it's made all
day long, but I never believe I really "own" a place
until I have walked the vineyards, met the winegrowers,
and gotten a personal "lay of the land," a sense of what
the French call *terroir*. In my opinion, that's the only
way a deeper understanding and connection with a
place can be made.

Travel is also valuable because it gives so many opportunities for common ground with the very diverse set of customers we see every day at Wines by Jennifer®. After all, who doesn't love trading travel stories about tasting their way through wine country, from Napa to Tuscany to Burgundy, and everywhere in between?

Of course, all this travel doesn't happen without collecting a few stories along the way...

12 Fifty before 50™

Fifty before 50™ is a phrase Don and I coined to describe a goal we set for ourselves of visiting all 50 United States before turning the age of 50. Catchy and clever (so we thought), it served as our mantra to keep us on target as we set about accomplishing this goal in earnest.

In fact, we came to love the idea of Fifty before 50™ so much that we trademarked it!

The project had its origins from a trip our son, Daniel, took several years ago which led him through several new (to him) states. During the course of discussing his impressions, he asked us how many of the 50 states we had visited.

Good question!

We each had been to a majority of them already by virtue of extensive travel in our professional careers up to that point.

I had plenty of experience flying myself in my trusty Piper Archer II to regions throughout North America calling on my clients for the consulting business I had created exclusively for that purpose in the mid-90s.

Don, meanwhile, had already traveled around much of the world himself taking care of business in positions of increasing responsibility during his 7-year career at Eastern Airlines.

And finally, as commercial pilots ferrying airplanes around the country, we both had ample opportunity to check several other "off the beaten path" states off the list.

So it became very clear that it would be far easier for us to answer Daniel's question by working backward and identifying those states we had *not* visited.

But in our world, goals must be clearly defined – it helps with focus.

So first, in determining what counted as "official" visited states, and for hitting the unvisited ones, the defining question became: *"What constitutes a visit?"*

We didn't want some token appearance like connecting in an airport to count, so we decided, quite logically we thought, that consuming an adult beverage (preferably at a local winery, brewery, or distillery, since we're always on the lookout for new WBJ® partners) on the ground outside the airport was sufficient.

So with that settled, what states were left?

Five states for Don: Alaska, Hawaii, Montana, Delaware, and North Dakota.

And four for me: Alaska, Hawaii, Vermont, and Rhode Island.

Because we had Alaska and Hawaii in common, those became the first targets.

Not a bad place to start!

These two exotic yet far-flung "bucket list" locations had somehow eluded us for the almost 50 years we had each spent on the planet.

With a goal in mind, however, we knocked 'em both off within a month of each other.

Ah, the power of goals!

Alaska was the first to fall. The beautiful 49th State remains to this day one of the most fascinating places

I've visited, which as of this writing totals *(teaser alert)* all 50 states, several Canadian provinces, and 58 countries spread across six continents.

(And the minute we hear of wine in Antarctica, it'll be seven.)

Don, for the record, has tallied all the above plus 11 additional countries, for a total of 69. (Looks like I may need to plan a secret solo trip to catch up!)

Beautiful, vast, and teeming with wildlife, Alaska was the great frontier I had always imagined it to be. I was so glad to have Daniel along with us to share the experience!

Daniel, Don, and I spent a month wandering around with our backpacks, beginning in Fairbanks and winding our way south eventually to Ketchikan. From the rugged beauty and the wildlife, to the quirkiness of the locals and the lifestyle built around general aviation, it was all very captivating to us.

But Don and I knew that the first question we'd get in our Tasting Room when we got back home would be: *"Is there wine in Alaska?!"*

In order to protect the "globetrotting wine experts" reputation we've earned, we knew we better have a good answer, so we got to work finding out.

We had heard rumors of wineries being located in all 50 states, but we honestly had our doubts about Alaska.

However, as the intrepid wine professionals we are, we were determined to find out for ourselves. And our persistence paid off.

Way down at the bottom of the Kenai peninsula, about 200 miles south of Anchorage, lies a town called Homer. Known as the "Halibut Fishing Capital of the World," Homer is also home to what was at the time the only winery in the entire state: Bear Creek Winery.

Figuring that a trip down the peninsula would be nothing if not beautiful, there really was only one course of action.

Road trip!

So in a rental car held partially together with, like so many things in Alaska, copious amounts of duct tape, off we went in search of Alaska wine. As expected, the drive was amazing. Stunning glacier views dominated the landscape, truly a sight that never got old.

At long last, we pulled into Homer, greeted by the typical Alaska welcoming committee of moose and bears. From the hill above town where the aptly named winery was located, we could see the famous Homer Spit, a 4 ½-mile stretch of sand and gravel that extends away from the mainland, kept intact by rock walls and human perseverance.

At Bear Creek Winery, the obvious challenges of viticulture in Alaska meant that any fermented grape juice they produced was made with fruit purchased elsewhere, but their wide range of other fruit and vegetable wines was very well done. The rhubarb was our favorite, both because it was local and because it was good!

Maybe my favorite thing about the winery was the hospitality. As service providers, we pay close attention when the tables are turned and we become service consumers. I'm not afraid to admit we've even "borrowed" a few ideas along the way when it was warranted, both as a "*we* should do this," and as a "we should definitely *not* do this."

But I'm pleased to say that Bear Creek passed our customer service test with flying colors!

Best of all, it just felt good to be able to say "been there, done that" with regard to Alaska wine. And although we didn't get the proverbial t-shirt, we do have the Bear Creek wine glasses at Wines by Jennifer® to prove that we made it to Alaska "wine country" still to this day!

Interestingly, Alaska was also where I had my very first exposure to "growlers," the glass jugs that allow for takeaway beer from breweries.

In those days, craft breweries were not as common as they are now, and growlers had yet to cross my radar.

Until I arrived in Haines.

Haines is a hidden gem of a town in the southeastern Alaska panhandle known for its large bald eagle migrations. It remains hidden because it is not a stop for the dozens of cruise ships plying the waters of the Inside Passage, ships we heard locals refer to dismissively as "floating incubators of disease."

It is a stop, however, on the Alaska Marine Highway, the ferry system that serves as the primary mode of transportation in this part of the state. Spartan but efficient, these ships had sleeping space, not in the way of private cabins, rather in the form of cots and blankets to spread out community-style on the main deck. Ample food options, better whale watching opportunities, and most importantly, access to adult beverages rounded out the experience.

A cruise ship it ain't, but it was our kind of ride. And ride it we did!

On this particular segment, we disembarked at the Haines ferry terminal and started working on Job One: finding a place to stay.

It wasn't long before we stumbled upon House No. 1 on Officer's Row, a bed-and-breakfast listed in the National Register of Historic Places. It sits right on the perimeter of one of the most interesting tourist sites in Haines, the old parade grounds of nearby Fort Seward.

And that's where we met Norm.

Norm was the gregarious and hilarious owner of House No. 1 on Officer's Row. Quick with a quip, a barb, or a hand, depending upon what he considered appropriate, he was easily one of the most colorful characters from a long list of candidates that we met while in Alaska.

As he immediately began regaling us with his tall tales and off-color jokes, I couldn't stop glancing at the generic brown glass containers that lined the shelves of the House No. 1 kitchen. There must have been over a dozen of them.

My curiosity finally got the best of me and I just had to ask him, "What are all those moonshine-looking jugs you've got everywhere?"

Norm seemed insulted at the question. "Seriously?" he barked, "You've never seen a growler?!"

Uh, sorry, Norm, I have not.

So he began to explain that they were containers used to store and transport fresh draft beer he sourced from the local brewery, Haines Brewing Company.

With about 17 of them in stock, it was apparent that he was quite a fan.

Norm went on to explain that the brewery was an easy bike ride from his b-and-b, and why didn't we take a couple growlers, hop on the bikes he had available for guests, and go pay Haines Brewing a visit?

An excellent idea indeed!

So we loaded up the growlers in our backpacks, hopped on the bikes, and armed with directions from Norm, off we went in search of some suds to fill our new toys.

Located on the site of the Southeast Alaska State Fairgrounds, Haines Brewing Company is one of Alaska's original craft breweries. It shares its space with the set of the Disney movie, "White Fang," which was filmed entirely in Haines in 1991.

Great setting, great people, growlers full of tasty beer ready for the ride home (their Spruce Tip Ale is the bomb!), what's not to love?

I'll tell you what. The ride home.

Bike rides in Alaska are great when they're downhill in the daylight and it's dry and you're sober. When they're uphill in dwindling light in the rain and you're, uh, not sober, let's just say the fun quotient is significantly diminished.

Thank goodness for the growlers!

Somewhere along the way on our ride back home, Don made the executive decision that we would be making a couple of intermediate stops to off-load excess weight. His logic was that by consuming the beer we had acquired, it would make the uphill pedaling a little less strenuous.

Not wanting to rain on his little parade, I reluctantly agreed, and we proceeded to drink the growlers back to their original empty condition so we could clean and replace them on Norm's shelf upon our return.

When we finally arrived back at House No. 1 and told Norm of our day, it was clear we had made him very proud.

The value of travel was impressed upon me yet again in Alaska, this time in an event that came with an extra helping of goosebumps.

Unbeknownst to me at the time, on Good Friday in 1964, the most powerful recorded earthquake in United States history occurred in the Prince William Sound about 75 miles east of Anchorage. Not only the largest in American history, it is also the second largest recorded earthquake ever, behind only a magnitude 9.5 quake that struck Chile in 1960.

This tragic event is now commemorated at Anchorage's Earthquake Park, located on the exact site where an entire neighborhood slid into the Cook Inlet during this catastrophic 4 ½-minute-long event.

It is a spot that soon became very memorable to me as well.

The park itself is a series of educational markers and signs situated along a large cliff that was created by the giant tsunami that struck the area shortly after the earthquake that fateful day.

But history aside, the setting at Earthquake Park also just happens to be an aviator's dream.

Start with the commanding views of the crystal blue waters of Cook Inlet and the downtown Anchorage skyline shimmering off in the distance.

Add to it the park's location just east of the departure end of Runway 33 at Ted Stevens Anchorage International Airport, where departing widebody aircraft flew so close over me that I almost felt the need to duck.

Complete the picture with the constant activity from the busiest seaplane base in the world, Lake Hood, located just a mile south, and I felt like I had died and gone to aviation heaven.

But just when I thought the experience could not possibly get any better, it was elevated to a whole new level when, seemingly out of nowhere, the United States Air Force Thunderbirds screamed across the distant horizon.

Unbeknownst to us, we had wandered into Earthquake Park right in the middle of Anchorage's biennial Arctic Thunder Air Show!

Don and I reveled in our good fortune for a moment, then we sat down and proceeded to enjoy the show from our bird's-eye perch.

Several years later, I was at the shoppe one day when a young couple came in to enjoy a wine tasting. When they were checking out, I happened to notice the gentleman had an Alaska driver's license.

Never wanting to miss an opportunity to connect with a customer, I mentioned how much we had loved our trip to Alaska. I then asked what part of Alaska he lived in, and he said Anchorage.

I then began to share my Earthquake Park experience with him (as I usually do when talking about Alaska), when he gave me this wide-eyed look and exclaimed, "That's the exact spot where I proposed to my wife!"

We shared a big smile and a common bond, and I gave thanks once again for the gift of travel.

Hawaii was knocked off our lists just a few short weeks later. It represented a continuation of a fun family tradition we had begun a few years earlier, the tradition of birthday travel.

Don and I abandoned the concept of physical gift-giving many years ago, not only for ourselves, but for

Daniel, too. We have long preferred experiences over objects, memories over material things.

And to us, there aren't many better experiences than travel. That's why birthdays in our family are now spent on the road at the destination of the celebrator's choosing.

One of my fondest memories was seeing the look of bewildered excitement on Daniel's young face when he unwrapped the box of oranges we had given him one Christmas. He was not yet old enough to understand the symbolism: we were bound for Miami on my birthday trip to watch our USC Trojans win the 2004 college football national championship with a convincing win over Oklahoma in the, you guessed it, 2005 *Orange* Bowl.

So when he had the chance to visit his 47th state while catching the Trojans in action again against Hawaii in Honolulu, the destination of choice for Don's 48th birthday trip was a foregone conclusion.

Montana was chosen in 2011 as the site of our annual week-long WBJ® Strategic Planning Retreat, a practice Don and I began back in 2005. Occurring annually in January, its sole purpose is to isolate ourselves so we can focus on "big picture" strategic business planning for Wines by Jennifer®. We always choose a relatively remote, cold-weather destination to reduce pesky distractions like sunshine and outdoor activities that would detract from our productivity.

This retreat would be strategic for two reasons. First, for the planning that would take place; second, for the elimination of state Number 48 on Don's rapidly dwindling list.

The 2011 version of our retreat was focused on putting the finishing touches on our WBJ® Operations Manual, which we had been developing on a continual basis since we opened in 2003. This rather voluminous 1,000+ page tome was the result of our almost OCD-like compulsion for structure and organization, driven not only by our corporate training, but also by our aviation training, with its mandatory use of checklists.

Try as we might though, we couldn't completely eliminate distractions. Not when you're within a stone's throw of two national forests, one national park, and the largest freshwater lake west of the Mississippi.

The Wines by Jennifer® Story

So while we did get out and enjoy a bit of the glorious Montana scenery, we mostly powered through and successfully completed our Manual, which is now serving us well as the linchpin of standardization for our Wines by Jennifer® operation.

Our commitment to Fifty before 50™ was probably never more on display than when Don crossed the penultimate state off his list.

We had just spent 43 days traversing five countries across the continent of South America on a crazy voyage Don had cooked up that seemed to me something like Marco Polo on steroids.

It began in Ecuador, with additional stops in the Galapagos Islands (still Ecuador), Peru, Chile, Easter Island (still Chile), and Argentina, before we finally concluded our own little Magical Mystery Tour in Uruguay.

It was an exhilarating yet grueling journey that left me longing for nothing more than a few nights spent at home in the comfort of my own bed.

Our long flight home included a layover of several hours in New York City, and I was looking forward to spending it relaxing in an airport lounge we had access to by virtue of the business class award tickets Don had secured via his usual creative methods.

Don, meanwhile, had other ideas.

As he was diligently working away on his iPad, I had the sneaking suspicion that he was up to something – as usual.

I cautiously asked, "What are you working on?" and he replied, "Train schedules."

Uh-oh.

Don had determined that if we hustled and experienced no hiccups, our schedule would allow for a quick detour to his Number 49: Delaware.

It was simple, Don assured me.

First, we would take a taxi from JFK airport to Penn Station in Manhattan. Then we would hop aboard the Acela Express bound for Philadelphia and points beyond, including the ever-popular tourist destination of Wilmington, Delaware.

Well, I must admit that I do always enjoy Amtrak. There is just something about "riding the rails" that appeals to both of us.

For Don, on this particular trip, a big part of that "something" was undoubtedly the Dogfish Head beer they were serving on board. Not yet available in the Midwest at the time, it was a "bucket list" brewery we eventually visited on a future, post-50 trip to Delaware.

But that's a story for our next book!

The forecast called for a beautiful day in Wilmington, and Don had already decided our two destinations. They sat conveniently co-located just a short 20-minute stroll from the train station along the banks of the Christina River.

A brewery and a ballpark.

Predictable.

Named for the hill outside nearby Newark, Delaware where a fierce Revolutionary War battle took place, Iron Hill Brewery has an impressive pedigree. They have thrice won the "World's Best Brewpub" award at Great American Beer Fest, in 2010, 2014, and 2016.

They have leveraged their success by expanding now to 16 locations across the Eastern Seaboard. Although opening additional Wines by Jennifer® locations was not in our plans, we were nevertheless inspired to hear their story as we enjoyed a flight of their tasty brews while overlooking the scenic Christina River.

Sufficiently hydrated, we then walked across the street and took a quick self-guided tour of Frawley Stadium, home of the Kansas City Royals Class A minor-league affiliate Wilmington Blue Rocks.

That stop coincidentally completed another list we had been working on: visit every Royals minor-league affiliate. This one came with an asterisk though, since we didn't actually see the Blue Rocks in action.

So with our mission accomplished, we paused for one last look around to let Delaware soak in, then headed for the train station.

Unlike Delaware, which was a "sequel" on the backend of our South America trip, my climactic 49th and 50th states of Vermont and Rhode Island were more like a "prequel," a kind of warm-up act to another one of our wild adventures that followed.

Don had been hard at work again, this time crafting an Australasian itinerary that would find us traveling from Vancouver to Perth, with intermediate stops in Hong Kong and Bali.

I was so excited to finally get to see all the Western Australia wine regions I'd only dreamed about until then.

But first, I was curious how Don planned to get us to Vancouver, not the easiest destination from Kansas City.

No problem, he said. We just had to go east a little ways first, via Vermont and Rhode Island, with a little dash of Long Island wine country on the side!

Although it appeared at first as though he might be a bit geographically challenged, I had learned to trust him in these matters.

As it just so happened, because the days were dwindling until my 50th birthday, Don had decided there was no way he was going to see me fall short of my Fifty before 50™ goal on his watch. So he had taken matters into his own hands and specifically set up our positioning flight to Vancouver out of JFK, providing a convenient excuse to begin our adventure in Albany, New York, of all places.

A curious selection under normal circumstances, but considering it provided a perfect starting point for a scenic drive through my final two states of Vermont and Rhode Island, followed by a car ferry to Long Island for some winery visits on the way to JFK, it couldn't have worked out any better.

And he did it all just for me.

So I was now officially a member of the Fifty before 50™ Club, but it was lonely at the top. It was time for my partner in crime to join me in the Club.

The grand finale of our joint Fifty before 50™ adventure to North Dakota was about to begin.

Ironically, North Dakota was one of the first states outside of Missouri that I had ever seen, but it was destined to be Magic Number 50 for Don.

It should probably come as no surprise by now that this trip started for us, naturally, in another country.

We flew into Calgary in late June, 2012, a mere two months shy of Don's 50th birthday.

After an all-too-brief visit to beautiful Lake Louise and Banff National Park, a UNESCO World Heritage Site, we reversed our track and headed back to the southern

Alberta town of Medicine Hat, which you may know is not a UNESCO World Heritage Site.

Med Hat, as it is known, is a small western prairie town called the "sunniest city in Canada." That sounded to me a bit like the being the "warmest city in Siberia," but it was pleasant enough for our three-day visit.

The purpose of this segment of the trip was to watch the son of one of Don's best friends, Kevin Dotson, play baseball for the Medicine Hat Mavericks of the Western Major Baseball League.

Bubba Dotson at the time was a collegiate baseball player at Missouri Western State University. He was spending his summer playing in this Canadian wood-bat "showcase" league where mostly American college players displayed their talents in hopes of making it to the professional ranks.

Don has had a very close bond with Bubba since the day he was born, so it was a special moment indeed for them both when we showed up in the Hat.

July 1st, Canada Day, dawned warm and sunny, and it was shaping up to be an absolutely perfect night for baseball. The Mavs were at home that night to face the Okotoks Dawgs in a key Western Division match-up.

It was Military Appreciation Night at Athletic Park, and the Mavs were decked out in their camouflage jerseys to honor the Canadian Armed Forces. These same jerseys were to be auctioned off for charity after the game.

After a couple of uneventful at-bats early in the game, Bubba came to the plate in the bottom of the 6th inning with the Mavs trailing by two.

The bases were loaded.

I'd like to add to the drama here with the story of a long and protracted at-bat, Bubba fighting off several foul balls to stay alive at the plate, but there was nothing of the sort.

Instead, the moment was over in a split second, but it will live forever in my memory.

That's because Bubba was looking first-ball fastball, and he got one.

It was a no-doubter the minute it left the bat. The packed house rose in unison and began to cheer. Don yelled so loud from his excitement that he literally had no voice for the next day and a half.

Then, after he had rounded the bases and entered the dugout, the chant began, *Bub-ba, Bub-ba, Bub-ba*, rising in volume until Bubba finally emerged for his triumphant curtain call.

You see, Bubba, with his outsized personality and hard-nosed play, had quickly become a crowd favorite in Medicine Hat just as he always had wherever he played.

I thought to myself at that very moment that *you just cannot make this stuff up*.

In the midst of the celebration, Don pulled out his phone to share the excitement with Kevin with what little voice he had left. Kevin was back in Kansas City watching the game on the internet, just as we had been doing at home all summer.

I was so happy they got to share that moment together.

After the game, Don ran downstairs to find the auction. He was bound and determined not to be outbid for Bubba's jersey, because he already had big plans for it.

Imagine his horror when he learned that all the jerseys, including Bubba's, had been auctioned off AFTER THE 7th INNING!

But Don would not be denied.

After some investigation to discover who had placed the winning bid, Don set about finding her (a female, of course!), and proceeded to plead his case for the jersey. He explained the whole situation, which most people would dismiss as the stuff of fantasy had they not just witnessed it themselves. He also made sure she understood that he certainly intended to make it worth her while to part with her trophy.

She would have nothing of it — the extra payment, that is. All she asked for was what she had invested, which Don was all too happy to give her.

Typical Canadian, eh?

You can just imagine the scene when we returned home later that month and Don presented to Kevin the very jersey his son was wearing when he hit his first career grand slam!

Later that night in Med Hat, Bubba, his girlfriend-now-bride Sabrina, Don, and I all piled into our rented convertible and drove to the Saamis Teepee (the world's largest teepee and a local landmark) for some Canada Day fireworks to close out the evening.

But as exciting as those fireworks turned out to be, they could never compare to the ones we had just witnessed.

Finally, it was time for North Dakota.

The Wines by Jennifer® Story

Our 4th of July flight from Calgary was bound for Minneapolis, where we planned to pick up our rental car and make the drive to whatever part of North Dakota was closest.

We chose the town of Wahpeton as our destination because of its location in the extreme southeastern part of the state.

All it would take there would be a sip of an adult beverage on *terra firma*, and maybe a picture by the road sign welcoming us to the state. With that accomplished, we intended to point our car south toward Parkville posthaste.

Easy in, easy out.

Instead, what we found waiting for us in North Dakota is a perfect illustration of why we've always considered spontaneity and flexibility to be important components of our travel strategy.

Upon arriving in Wahpeton, we learned there was a decades-long tradition for the local American Legion baseball team to play its cross-river Minnesota rival, Breckenridge, as part of a day-long celebration of America's birthday.

Because we're baseball fans, and because it was getting too late to drive nine hours down I-29 to get home, we decided if we had to spend the night somewhere, this was as good a place as any. After all, Don had waited a long time for this day.

We made arrangements for a room for the night, picked up a bottle of American bubbly to celebrate the occasion, and settled in with the townsfolk in the bleachers to enjoy a slice of small-town holiday Americana.

The game started under bright blue skies and warm temperatures, but it began to get dark and a little cool sometime around the middle innings, revealing a starry night unpolluted by light.

It was North Dakota, after all.

I don't even remember who won the game, but it didn't really matter. I was just happy to enjoy a wonderful summer evening of baseball, and more importantly, welcome Don to the Club!

Right as we were preparing to leave, the lights went down, revealing a spotlight focused on a huge American flag flying majestically from a flagpole located behind the outfield fence.

It was clearly not yet time to leave.

Don hustled to the car and retrieved the sparkling wine and our trusty WBJ® swirl cups *(don't leave home without 'em!)*, and we settled back in to enjoy the show.

As the loudspeakers began pumping out patriotic John Phillip Sousa tunes (doubly appropriate due to the little-known fact that Don once played the tuba), the fireworks began exploding over Old Glory as a magnificent, bright orange full moon began to rise slowly above the horizon.

Don and I then shared a toast of bubbly made right in the good ole U.S. of A., a toast not only to Don's 50th state, but also to this great land we call home.

And I sure hope he won't mind me saying so, but while all this magic was happening right in front of us, I glanced over at Don and couldn't help but notice a trace of a tear in his eye.

Turns out I might've had one, too.

Even though the age of 50 is now well in our rearview mirror, the concept of Fifty before 50[™] continues to live on long after we completed it.

It's always exciting for me to witness people hearing our Fifty before 50[™] stories and be so inspired that they decide to make it a personal goal for themselves.

So it is my sincere hope that, regardless of age, the stories you have just read will inspire you to one day visit all 50 states in this beautiful land, too, if you haven't already!

13 Playing "The Game"

As I mentioned before, Don and I both have always loved to travel. We're pilots, after all.

But unlike most things in our lives, we didn't *intentionally* set out to become known for our exotic, frequent, and extended global adventures.

That one kinda just happened by accident.

And it happened largely as a result of Don's deep dive down the rabbit hole of a cult-like hobby many refer to as travel "hacking."

Don, however, always preferred the term travel "game." To him, hacking implied something shady, illegal, or underhanded, things that would not fit within his code of ethics.

A game, on the other hand, is a competition where you keep score and play by the rules.

All completely legal, ethical, and legitimate.

With Don's competitive nature and background in the airline industry, he was a natural at it. And like most hobbies these days, there are also plenty of online resources that Don used to fill in any gaps he might have had – not that there were many.

I can attest that he was quite a student of "The Game."

The way to win at this game, as he described it to me, was twofold:

1. Accumulate as many assets (miles and points) as possible using as many of the tools available for doing so as possible.

2. Leverage those assets in the most effective way by finding undervalued properties ("sweet spot" redemptions) in the various loyalty programs.

Sounded a lot like business to me.

According to Don, loyalty programs are notorious for changing rules and currency values at a moment's notice, much like Lucy pulling the football from Charlie Brown.

A rumored threat of a rule change or a devaluation is usually what sprung him into action.

The typical planning scenario for one of our trips was as easy (for me anyway) as 1, 2, 3:

The Wines by Jennifer® Story

1. Don would come to me and ask if we could get away for a certain block of time.

2. I would check our schedule at the shoppe for private parties, special events, team member vacation schedules, and so on, and feed him dates we could get away.

3. He would then hole up in his office for hours on end like a mad scientist, crafting the perfect itinerary based on whatever sweet spot it was that was disappearing and whatever award availability there was for the dates we could go.

Then, like completing a giant puzzle, Don would begin sorting through all the variables and putting the pieces together. His task was made more difficult by his refusal to fly economy, a leftover from his days flying only first class as an airline executive.

Who was I to argue? All it cost was a few more miles.

Slowly but ever-so-surely, something recognizable would begin to take shape, the progress indicated to me by the ratio of cheers to groans coming from his office.

I distinctly remember late nights listening to Don spoon-feed airline agents the routings of complex itineraries he had already researched and constructed using various tools he had, both free and paid.

Little did the agent on the other side of the call know who they were dealing with. Don had been living and breathing this stuff for years.

It was fascinating to watch.

Ultimately, positively beaming from his success, he would emerge victorious and deliver to me a printed calendar with all the relevant flight information.

It was like a Rubik's Cube of information such as airline codes (because seemingly every segment was on a different airline), departure and arrival cities and times, flight numbers and such.

The finished product was suitable for framing, not that I could, because I needed it with me at all times just to keep track of where I was and where I was going.

Our itineraries were usually very, shall we say, "active."

Don't believe me?

Here's a month-long around-the-world trip we took in 2013:

- MCI-ORD-YUL-ZRH-VIE-IST-PVG-ICN-NRT-ORD-MCI

In plain English, that's Kansas City to Chicago to Montreal to Zurich to Vienna to Istanbul to Shanghai to Seoul to Tokyo to Chicago to Kansas City.

All done with miles.

That trip was filled with memorable moments, as you would expect. But one that stands out to me, because Don reminds me of it at every opportunity, is the infamous glass of Chinese wine I had at the rooftop bar at the Peninsula Hotel in Shanghai.

The Peninsula is a beautiful hotel overlooking Shanghai's famous Bund. We were staying at a lovely place ourselves not far away that had perfect views of their rooftop bar.

It all looked very inviting, and we promised ourselves we would pay a visit at least once in the nine days we were there.

Finally, on our next-to-last day, we made it to the Peninsula.

It was splendid!

The air was reasonably clear (for Shanghai, that is), the atmosphere was inviting, the views to die for.

Don asked for the wine list with an eye on sampling the local products, as we always do. There were two Chinese wines, a white and a red.

The glasses were priced in Chinese Yuan Renminbi, so Don pulled out his phone and plugged the numbers into his currency converter app.

He announced that it looked like the white was the equivalent of around $7 and the red, interestingly, looked to be $43.

I told him that must be a mistake, that maybe he punched it in wrong on his app.

Don took the safe route and ordered the white. I was in the mood for red, so ignoring Don's warnings, I ordered it. A Cabernet as I recall.

The bill and the wine came together shortly thereafter, the moment of truth upon us.

I glanced at the bill, then I glanced at Don, then I proceeded to drink every last drop of the most vile, disgusting $43 glass of wine I'll ever have in my life.

Here's another doozy from 2014, this one being a fine example of Don's willingness to travel 180° in the opposite direction of the final destination just so he could fly in the "proper" cabin:

The Wines by Jennifer® Story

- MCI-EWR-JFK-ICN-HAN-BKK-SYD-CHC-
  AKL-SYD-BKK-TPE-ICN-JFK-LGA-DCA-
  IAD-MCI

Decoded, that's Kansas City to Newark to Kennedy to
Seoul to Hanoi to Bangkok to Sydney to Christchurch
to Auckland to Sydney to Bangkok to Taipei to Seoul to
Kennedy to LaGuardia to Reagan National to Dulles to
Kansas City.

That's an actual trip, folks, with stopovers of varying
lengths all along the way.

Again, completely done with miles.

(Don made good use of the co-terminal technique here,
which just means flying into one airport and out of
another in the same city. It's a positioning trick that can
help when award availability is tight.)

That trip was noteworthy for many reasons, not the
least of which was our visit with Kevin Judd in
Marlborough on the South Island of New Zealand.

It was also memorable for what happened after we left
Marlborough.

Nelson, also on the South Island west of Marlborough,
is well known for its natural beauty: golden beaches,
pristine forests, and rugged mountains.

It also claims to be the sunniest region in New Zealand.

Unless you're in a cyclone, that is.

The rain from Cyclone Louise was blowing sideways so hard you could barely see three feet in front of you, but we soldiered on, because seriously, how often do you get to New Zealand?

But then again, we seem to have a tendency to attract calamities and natural disasters in our travels.

The laundry list is lengthy:

- *two earthquakes in Chile*
- *an earthquake in California*
- *a Scirocco windstorm in Sicily*
- *locusts in the south of France*
- *a hurricane in South Florida*
- *wildfires in South Africa*

I'm probably forgetting a couple.

So who are we to cry over a little cyclone in New Zealand?

The Kiwis certainly didn't. It was amazing, actually.

Every tasting room and restaurant we went to that day was not only open, they were packed. Intrepid New Zealanders everywhere, all enjoying their regular Sunday outings as usual.

The farmers were all out, too, tending to their lambs and goats and grapes and just getting their jobs done.

It was a good reminder for us that, despite what life sometimes throws at you, at the end of the day, the show must go on.

Of course, like many hobbies, there are also "secret societies" for which membership requires a certain code or level of expertise just to gain access. These codes are not for sale, instead they're earned only through experience.

The travel game is no different, and it just so happened that Don had one such code.

That's how we found ourselves in Turkey twice in three months in the summer of 2015, intent on burning through the stash of miles we had accumulated before that particular option disappeared.

No problem for us, though, because we had been to Turkey before and absolutely loved it. The people, the food, the wine, the natural beauty, all wonderful.

(And the raki! We loved this anise-based spirit so much that we immediately added it to our spirits menu at the shoppe when we got back home. *We're working!)*

I highly recommend you visit Turkey if you've never been.

In case you're curious, the routing for these two trips looked like this:

1. MCI-MDW-PHL-YYZ-FRA-SAW-ASR-ADB-SAW-FRA-YYZ-LGA-MCI

2. MCI-LGA-JFK-BRU-FRA-SAW-IST-ERC-SAW-FRA-YYZ-BUF-BWI-MCI

(Now that you have practice, your assignment is to decode this alphabet soup for yourself!)

While there are *plenty* of wild adventures from both trips, this particular story took place on the first one.

Kuşadası [koo-SHAH-duh-suh] is a major resort town and cruise port on Turkey's Aegean coast. It's best known as the "jumping off" point to nearby Ephesus, the best-preserved ancient city in the eastern Mediterranean.

We enjoyed exploring the area, especially Ephesus. It is simply a phenomenal place that you really have to see to believe.

But in the back of our minds, beckoning a short 1 ½ miles offshore from Kuşadası, was the Greek island of Samos. With easy access via an hour-long ferry ride, we couldn't pass up the chance to add another stamp to our passports.

(Speaking of passports, I'll never forget the look on the South Africa customs official's face the day he inspected mine and deadpanned, "Wow, Jenny, you get around.")

As an added bonus, Samos is covered in grapevines. It is famous for its sweet Muscat dessert wines that are exported around the world.

Wine is such a big deal there that they even boast their own Samos Wine Museum.

There is only one round-trip ferry per day, leaving at 9am and returning at 5pm, so for once, our planning process was made pretty simple.

So with ferry tickets in hand, we hopped aboard and sailed off to our next adventure.

The plan was to first take a spin through the wine museum near the ferry terminal, then rent a car and spend the day wandering the steep, vine-covered hillsides of the island. Maybe we'd even find a winery or two before catching our return ferry.

So far, so good.

After visiting the museum, we rented our car and began the long, scenic climb up the mountain. Reaching the top, we paused to admire the view.

And what a view it was!

Bright blue skies, surrounded by grapevines, the deep blue Aegean Sea glistening in the background, what's not to love?

After a few hours exploring, it was time to start making our way to the terminal for the ferry ride back to the Turkish mainland.

GPS coverage was spotty and we had been relying on signage to get around. The island is not huge, so it hadn't been a problem so far.

We came upon an intersection on the side of the mountain where we saw two signs pointing in opposite directions.

Both read "Ferry Terminal." Neither looked appealing.

Meanwhile, Don channeled his inner Yogi Berra: "If you come to a fork in the road, take it."

Not finding the humor in the situation, I flipped the proverbial coin and picked one.

As we carried on down the side of the mountain, the "road" was getting a little narrower, a little steeper, and a little bumpier with each tire rotation.

And they weren't rotating very quickly, either, because this "road" was becoming littered with boulders that had succumbed to gravity, making our passage increasingly difficult.

In fact, the road had become so narrow that turning around was no longer an option. The prospect of backing up the direction we had just come from was equally unattractive.

Eventually, we came upon a tiny village. Finally, I thought, an oasis in this hillside odyssey.

Not so fast my friend.

Once in the village, the road became so narrow, the turns so tight, that it began to look less like a road and more like a walking path.

Forward movement was soon no longer an option, so we attempted what was approximately a 37-point turn to escape.

No luck. We were stuck, wedged literally between a rock and a hard place.

In dire situations such as these, Don always had a fallback solution.

Beer.

He had spied a little *taverna* and thought a brief reboot might be in order. Time was running short, but not having any better ideas, I agreed.

While sipping our beer and contemplating our options, we decided to try to enlist the assistance of the locals.

We explained our plight the best we could, and the only gentleman who could understand us at all informed us we had just arrived in his little village via donkey path.

Perfect.

However, this wasn't the first time he'd seen it, he said, if that was any consolation.

It wasn't.

Time was quickly becoming a factor, so Don asked the gentleman if he might come take a look at our predicament and see what could be done.

He agreed, so I waited alone patiently in the taverna with my beer while the Greek patrons eyed me sympathetically.

Don returned after about 45 minutes with the verdict.

Good news, he said. The car is out.

Bad news, he said. The ferry has sailed.

And thus was introduced into our travel lexicon the new phrase "donkey path."

Invoked by one of us to the other whenever it becomes obvious a poor decision has been made, proper usage includes:

- *"I'm not sure this is the right donkey path."*

- *"What was your logic behind choosing this donkey path?"*

- And my personal favorite, the simple, yet brutally effective, *"Nice donkey path."*

So it was with cold beer in our hands surrounded by our new Greek friends that we watched as our ferry sailed slowly away from the harbor and out of our view.

We could've stressed over the fact that we now would have two hotel rooms for the same night in two different countries, or that we had fresh rental car damage to pay for, or that we had two more ferry tickets to buy.

All of which would be categorized later under a special accounting line item we had created especially for these occasions labeled "Stupid Tax."

But we didn't.

Instead, we preferred to remember the generosity and helpful spirit of the new friends we had just made.

That, and just how good those Greek beers tasted.

See, it's really all in how you look at things.

Part Five

THE FUTURE

14 When Everyone's Zigging, It's Time to Zag

First things first. What's with the "zig-zag" title, you may ask?

Well, I just wanted to include that line in this book somewhere, because I have always lived my life that way. And a conversation about the future of Wines by Jennifer® seemed like as good a place as any.

The first time I heard the phrase "when everyone's zigging, it's time to zag" was from serial entrepreneur Brian Clark, founder of the content marketing website Copyblogger.

To me it means one thing: don't be a follower.

I've been a contrarian my entire life. Swimming upstream, taking the path of what I call *best* resistance, doing what's right, not what's easy.

Zagging when others zig.

And that's what I'm about to do again.

While other people in my age group are zigging their way toward retirement, I'm zagging my way toward my next adventure, which I can assure you is *not* retirement.

I take that back. Actually, I retired a long time ago.

I just did it according to my favorite definition of the subject, courtesy of famous entrepreneurial success coach Dan Sullivan.

Dan's definition of retirement is "retiring from the things you don't want to do."

So, yeah, in that respect, I guess I'm officially retired.

But what do I *want* to do?

That's easy.

Continue to help people!

- *Help people have fun.*

- *Help people escape.*

- *Help people connect.*

In other words, continue to do the same things we've been doing at Wines by Jennifer® for going on 18 years now.

But in full disclosure between us friends, there are two groups of people that I feel we have "underserved" over the years, a situation that has been a source of frustration to me for some time.

These two groups are:

1. Those who were past members of the Wines by Jennifer® family, but are no longer because they have moved away.

2. Those we have met on our travels around the world who would love to be part of the Wines by Jennifer® family, but are too distant to practically do so.

So we have recently developed a plan to better serve not only those two groups, but also all the other members of our ever-growing WBJ® family that I'm excited to share with you!

It's simple, really.

We have begun to aggressively invest in and implement new tools and technology that now allow us to deliver a much more broad, diverse, and robust range of products both physical and digital for the benefit of our WBJ® family no matter how near or how far they may be.

These online resources are rich with exclusive and proprietary content such as a private forum moderated by me personally, podcasts with industry influencers, wine country videos produced from onboard our very own aircraft, ebooks, webinars, and various wine country contests, promotions, discounts, and recommendations. It's a treasure trove of information at your fingertips anytime day or night that will help you enjoy an authentic global wine country experience like never before!

None of this is necessarily revolutionary in today's day and age of course, unless maybe you're an "old school" global wine boutique that has always valued high-touch over hi-tech.

Of course it's important to note that this "updating of the ante" *(H/T: Flavor Flav!)* has been made possible only because of how well Daniel has assumed responsibility for the day-to-day management of the Wines by Jennifer® operation.

Without that, Don and I would never have been able to completely focus on the "big picture" strategic vision that we have developed for the shoppe, one that ensures Wines by Jennifer® will continue to be a pillar of downtown Parkville for years to come.

So yes, while we're very excited for our new innovations and offerings, we're more excited that, thanks to Daniel, we can *all* rest easy knowing that the #nextgen (or is it #next*jenn*?) is securely in place.

Additional Resources

At Last! Wines By Jennifer® Unveils New Website That Now Helps People *Around The World* Enjoy An Authentic Global Wine Country Experience From The Comfort Of Their Own Home!

This Resource Is for You If You Want Instant Access to Exclusive "Insider Secrets" from Experienced Wine & Travel Professionals <u>without</u> Investing Valuable Time & Money Learning Them Yourself!

Don't delay, visit www.WinesByJennifer.com right now while it's fresh in your mind to see our exciting new online experience for yourself!

Index

9/11 3, 10, 12

A

Ahlmann, Kaj 76-81

Air Race Classic 98

Andersen, Morten 73-75

Angel Flight Central 92-93

Aoki, Nori 91

B

Backsberg Estate Cellars 52

Bear Creek Winery 107-108

Berra, Yogi 143

Bize, Domaine Simon 87

Bize, Patrick 87

Bryant Family Vineyards 74-75

Burroughs 33

C

Café des Amis 40

California-Davis, University of 80

Capistrano 42

Central Missouri, University of 7

Clark, Brian 151

Cloudy Bay 57

Coulter, Mark 20

D

Daniel 13, 16, 30, 34, 62, 76, 103-104, 106, 116, 154

Danube River Wine Cruise, Wines by Jennifer's 101

DiPlacito, Tony 66

Dogfish Head 120

Dotson, Bubba 124-127

Dotson, Kevin 124, 126-127

Drucker, Peter 37

E

Earhart, Amelia Birthplace Museum 92

Eastern Airlines 32-33, 104

Edelston, Marty 64

Ellis, Richard 59

F

Five Man Electrical Band 39

Flavor Flav 154

Freedom Properties 29

Frost, Doug 35, 44

G

General Electric 76

Greywacke 57-59

H

Haines Brewing Company 111

Harms, Jay 20

Hedrick's 15-16

Hill, Napoleon 34

I

Ibis 65

Iron Hill Brewery 120

J

Jefferson Cup, The 64

Jennifer, THE 82-83

Jones, Loretta 99

Judd, Kevin 57-59, 138

Judd, Kimberley 59

K

Kansas City Royals 91, 121

Kauffman, Ewing Greater Kansas City Fund 92

Kennedy, Dan 7

Kremer, Ken and Lisa 73

Kroc, Ray 45

Kurtz, Brian 7, 93

M

Maine Beechcraft 4

March Madness 48

Mauch, Alan 76-77

McCarthy, Ken 7, 36

McDonald's 45

Miura, Ichiro and Emiko 68, 84-91

157

N

Northwest Missouri State University 33

O

Oktoberfest 56, 58-59

P

Park University 34

Perez, Perry 3-5

Perry, Bill 3

Pinot 48

Price-Waterhouse 55

R

Rimann, Marshall 19

S

Select Air Group, Inc. 4, 6, 14

Six Sigma 76-77, 80-81

Smith, Paul 72-73

Sperry 33

Stanley Cup 55

Strong, Rodney 60

Sullivan, Dan 152

Szalay, Al and Teri 28

T

Think and Grow Rich 34

Toad Hollow Vineyards 59-61

U

Unisys 33

USC Trojans 116

V

Vermeil, Dick 72-75

W

WBJ® Virtual Tasting 59-61

Welch, Jack 76

Williams, Frankie 60-61

Williams, Robin 60

Williams, Todd 60

Wind Shift Brewing 66

Wines by Jennifer's Wine March Madness™ 49, 52, 54, 56, 85

Jennifer and Don Stanton are the proprietors of Wines by Jennifer®, a unique luxury entertainment destination that has been helping people enjoy an authentic global wine country experience in historic downtown Parkville, Missouri since 2003.

As commercial pilots and serial travelers, they have visited all 50 states and scores of countries across six continents in their never-ending quest to discover the very best the world has to offer in food, wine, beer, and spirits, along with the fascinating people and stories that come with them.

Made in USA - Kendallville, IN
1089949_9781732850125
04.23.2020 1134